The First Americans

CALIFORNIA INDIANS

C. L. Keyworth

☑ **Facts On File**
New York • Oxford

About *The First Americans* Series:

This eight-volume series presents the rich and varied cultures of the many Native American tribes, placing each within its geographical and historical context. Each volume covers a different cultural area, providing an understanding of all the major North American Indian tribes in a systematic, region-by-region survey. The series emphasizes the contributions of Native Americans to American culture, illustrating their legacy in striking photographs within the text and in all-color photo essays.

California Indians

Facts On File, Inc.
460 Park Avenue South
New York NY 10016
USA

Facts On File Limited
Collins Street
Oxford OX4 1XJ
United Kingdom

Library of Congress Cataloging-in-Publication Data

Keyworth, C.L. (Cynthia L.)
    California Indians / C.L. Keyworth
      p.   cm. — The First Americans series
    Includes index.
    Summary: Examines the history, culture, changing fortunes, and
current situation of the various Indian peoples of California.
    ISBN 0-8160-2386-7
    1. Indians of North America—California—Juvenile literature.
[1. Indians of North America—California.]
I. Title   II. Series.
E78.C15K48 1991
979.4'00497—dc20   90–45543

A British CIP catalogue record for this book is available from the British Library.

Facts On File books are available at special discounts when purchased in bulk quantities for businesses, associations, institutions or sales promotions. Please call our Special Sales Department in New York at 212/683-2244 (dial 800/322-8755 except in NY, AK or HI) or in Oxford at 865/728399.

Design by Carmela Pereira
Jacket design by Donna Sinisgalli
Typography & composition by Tony Meisel

10 9 8 7 6 5 4 3 2 1

This book is printed on acid-free paper.
Manufactured in MEXICO.

▲ A Tolowa woman in traditional clothing.

CONTENTS

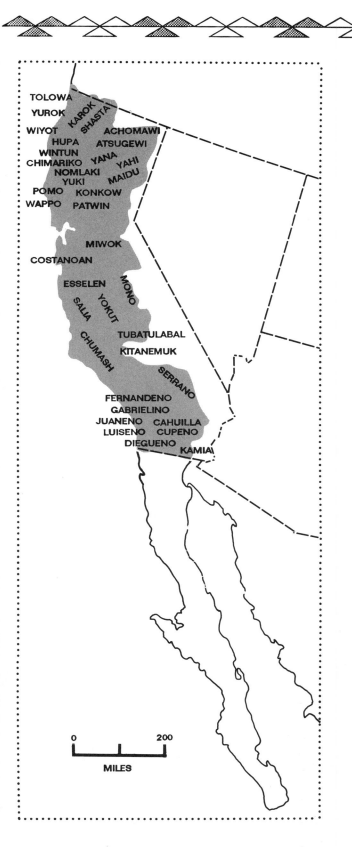

TOLOWA
YUROK
KAROK
WIYOT SHASTA
ACHOMAWI
HUPA ATSUGEWI
WINTUN
CHIMARIKO YANA
NOMLAKI YAHI
YUKI MAIDU
POMO KONKOW
WAPPO PATWIN

MIWOK
COSTANOAN
ESSELEN MONO
SALIA YOKUT
CHUMASH TUBATULABAL
KITANEMUK
SERRANO
FERNANDENO
GABRIELINO
JUANENO CAHUILLA
LUISENO CUPENO
DIEGUENO
KAMIA

0   200
MILES

THE CALIFORNIA CULTURE AREA

The approximate traditional tribal boundaries of the California culture area are shown in the larger map, with modern state boundaries. The smaller map shows the culture area in relation to all of North America.

▲ Fish were an important food source. Here a Yurok fisherman in the 1920s uses a long-handled dip net while standing on a platform built over a river.

CHAPTER ONE

ROOTS

Fifteen thousand years ago, at the end of the last Ice Age, the mountains and the high valleys of California were covered with glaciers. The climate was cool and moist, and what are now deserts were then plains dotted with hundreds of lakes. Huge mammals like the mammoth, the saber-toothed cat, the giant sloth, the mastodon, and the giant bison roamed the chilly landscape.

There is little evidence of early humankind in this period of California history. If Indians were in California then, they survived enormous changes in their environment. Between 14,000 and 10,000 years ago, the glaciers retreated and their melting waters raised the sea level. Warmer temperatures dried up lakes in the low-lying areas, deserts were formed, and the giant mammals died out. What evolved is the California that we know today—a land with moderate temperatures and mixed woodlands, grassy valleys, and deserts. Indians probably made their way into California from the rest of the North America about 10,000 to 8,000 years ago.

Once settled, Indians were more or less cut off from tribes outside California by the area's many natural barriers. To the north are the ancient lava flows and high, cold plains of the Modoc Plateau. The Cascade Range and Klamath Mountains rise in the north and the Coast and Transverse ranges form a chain down and across the state. To the west is the vast Pacific Ocean and a coastline often beaten with winds and heavy storms and hidden by dense fog. The high peaks of the Sierra Nevada range are covered with snow many months of the year, while its eastern side forms a steep, sheer wall. To the south are large stretches of barren wasteland and scorching deserts, like the Mojave Desert, the Great Basin, and Death Valley. All these barriers reduced friendly exchanges such as trade and communication as well as keeping out hostile or aggressive Indians. As a result, the California Indians remained fairly isolated for thousands of years.

In every area in which the Indians settled—the lush central valley, the coastal areas, the foothills, the deserts—they learned to use the resources in their environment to feed, shelter, clothe, and entertain themselves. The land was threaded with many small streams and larger rivers, which gave water for drinking, processing food, cooking, and washing. In many places, large forested areas provided timber for building and wood for fires. In the foothills and forests, there were huge groves of oak trees bearing edible acorns. The coastal waters, tidelands, rivers, and

lakes were teeming with salmon, trout, clams, oysters, mussels, otters, and sea lions. The valleys and plains offered a year-round and changing menu of seeds, fruits, berries, herbs, insects, and small game. Larger game roamed through the woodlands. Even the bare-looking and barren desert offered small game, cactus fruit, mesquite beans, insects, and—when watered—cultivated plants.

In order to survive, an intimate knowledge of the environment was essential. Each tribal member knew his or her natural world very well. The acorn harvester or seed gatherer, usually a woman, knew where the most productive plants grew. She knew which oak trees gave the best acorns. She knew where the dove weed, which attracted plump doves, grew. She discovered the best sites for finding wild berries or fields of new green clover. She knew where the willow trees grew and the tule rushes to make baskets. The hunters, too, found the deer trails and discovered which streams had plentiful fish.

In order to take full advantage of their environments, most Indian groups inhabited territories that included more than one life zone. They practiced limited migration, moving seasonally to where the food supply was. For example, in the fall many Indians moved from their main village up into the hills and camped there while they harvested acorns. Other groups dispersed in the spring to collect ripening greens and fresh roots and again in the fall to gather fruits, seeds, and nuts.

Most anthropologists divide California's Indian tribes into several groups in which tribes shared cultural lifeways. California Indians were isolated not only from other Indians but also from each other. As a result, they kept or developed their own distinct languages. Most Indian tribes could not understand the languages of their neighbors. There are more diverse languages among California Indians than in any other part of the country—about 60 separate languages and more than 100 dialects.

LIFEWAYS OF THE TRIBES

In northwest California, Hupa, Yurok, Shasta, Tolowa, and Wiyot Indians lived primarily along rivers, streams, bays, and ocean. They depended on the plentiful salmon and other fish for their main food source and developed a fishing technology of beautifully made boats, harpoons, and fishing weirs.

▲ Salmon was an important food fish for the Hupa of northeastern California. The area is mountainous and threaded with streams. Here a Hupa boy poses with a spear used to catch salmon.

Northeastern tribes such as the Modoc and Atsugewi lived on the high barren elevations of the Modoc Plateau and the Cascade Mountains. Both salmon and acorns were scarce, and the people hunted small game such as rabbits and gathered a tuber plant called the epos root. They developed an ingenious method of capturing deer by digging pits along the river and hiding the pits with branches. Later, when the horses of white fur trappers fell into these pits, the river was dubbed the "Pit."

Central California offered an abundant supply of resources as well as a temperate climate. Three-fifths of all California Indians lived in this area. These Indians gathered acorns from huge groves of oaks; they hunted, fished, and gathered plants. Tribes in the area included the Miwok, Maidu, Yokut, Costanoan, Esselen, and Pomo.

The Great Basin area was the poorest in resources and the least populated area of the state. It seldom rained, the summers were hot and dry,

▲ This beautiful Yokut basket combines feathers, dyed materials, and different weaving techniques.

and food was scarce. Life in the Great Basin was characterized by a constant search for food. Tribes such as the Mono and Northern Paiute moved often in order to find new supplies of seasonal food, traveling to grasslands when grass seed was ripe and to pinyon groves when the pine nuts could be harvested. They also hunted bighorn sheep and small game, and they ate insects. Their mobile life meant that their possessions had to be simple and lightweight enough to carry them on their backs. They had baskets for gathering and drying seeds, bows and arrows, and rabbit fur blankets for cold nights on the high desert.

In southern California, coastal-dwelling Indians such as the Chumash were accomplished fishers and skilled boat builders. To the east and south, southern desert dwellers such as the Gabrielino, Diegueno, and Cahuilla hunted small game, captured insects, and gathered fruit from the mesquite tree, the fan palm, and many different cactuses. Lacking abundant plant fibers, these Indians used the clay found in riverbeds to make pots and became better pottery makers than basket weavers.

Along the Colorado River, Yuma and Mojave Indians constituted the only true agricultural society in California, utilizing the rich floodplain area of the Colorado to plant corn, squash, beans, and pumpkins. The Yuma and the Mojave tribes were more likely to go to war than other tribes and would sometimes travel for a week or more to reach an enemy tribe. A specially trained class of warriors was armed with mesquite-wood clubs as well as bows and arrows. If they were victorious they took both scalps and captives.

Throughout all of California, the staple foods were acorns and fish. Indians saw the land-scape—animals and plants, even rocks and trees and mountains—as having feelings and thoughts, just as humans did.

Although Indians didn't "own" the land, they respected property rights—such as the right to fish in a certain section of the river or to gather acorns from a section of the oak forest. Indian tribes increased their food supply through trade or barter.

LIVING ON THE LAND

Finding food was the responsibility of the entire family or tribe, including women, men, and children. Through a rough division of labor, men hunted and fished and women harvested the acorn crop, gathered other plant foods, and fished for shellfish. This division of labor carried over to other tasks. Men were responsible for making the hunting tools and weapons and building fishing boats. Women constructed food storage buildings, stored and processed the plant harvests, and prepared the food.

In the days before white people came, California was full of natural orchards of oaks; seven kinds of oak trees grow in central California. Each tribe had its own oak groves within its territory and an individual family might put its own ownership mark on several trees. A single large oak tree produces an annual acorn crop of between 500 to 1,000 pounds a year, which means that one tribe's oak grove could produce over 100,000 pounds of acorns.

The harvesting season lasted for only a short time each fall, and so for several weeks the women went into the groves from sunup to sundown, gathering the fallen acorns from the ground and shaking the ripe fruit from the trees. Woven baskets were used to carry and hold the acorns. To store quantities of acorns for long periods of time, women made granaries of large storage baskets. These were hung from poles or trees to prevent spoilage and reduce damage from rodents and insects.

Although an excellent source of nutrition, acorns contain a bitter chemical, called tannin. Indian women developed a process to remove the tannin and make the acorn edible. They first ground the acorn meat into a flour, using a flat stone, then placed the flour in a shallow depression in the sand and rinsed it repeatedly with hot water. After seven or eight rinsings, the tannin was removed from the acorn flour.

Sometimes the flour was made into a flat piece of bread and baked in the fire, but more often it was simply made into a thick porridge by combining it with water in a cooking basket. Hot stones were dropped into the basket to cook the mixture, which was something like cooked cereal. Indians usually ate this food plain, although bits of meat were sometimes mixed in or berries or honey added as sweeteners.

Tribes who lived on or near waterways took in quantities of fish for food. Salmon, a seasonal favorite for coastal Indians like the Chumash, was caught when it was "running"—that is, when the salmon left the ocean waters and traveled up rivers and streams to spawn, or lay eggs. Salmon runs occurred twice a year, in the spring and, to a lesser extent, in the fall.

Nets were used to catch salmon and other fish such as whitefish, rainbow trout, and perch. Some Indians such as the Pomo wove fish traps that looked like long conical baskets. Swimming with the current, fish swam into the basket's opening and then couldn't swim out. Other tribes built fish-catching weirs—fences of stakes or brushwood—across streams. The fishers then speared the fish trapped by the weir. Usually, the weir was a temporary construction that would be taken down after a few days so that tribes further up the river could participate in the salmon harvest. This wasn't done out of generosity, but because infringing on another tribe's fishing supply might result in a conflict.

Coastal waters supplied shellfish, such as abalone, clams, mussels, oysters, and sea urchins. These shellfish were added to soups or cooked in coals or hot ashes until they opened, much as oysters are roasted today. When dead whales washed up on the beach, the Indians used both the meat for food and the whalebone for tools and decorations.

While most coastal Indians fished from the shore, some used boats. In the northwest, Indians built dugout canoes to navigate the swift Klamath River. Redwood or cedar trees were killed by burning them at the base. After the trees fell, Indians used sharp tools made from mussel shells to hollow out the log and smooth the interior. The Pomo and Yokut lake-dwelling

TULE RUSHES

Tule rushes—waterproof and lightweight—were used to make small boats. Tule's ability to shed water also made it a good choice for baskets, roofs, shoes, and sleeping mats.

tribes built raftlike canoes of tule rush or of lightweight balsa, which they propelled along the lakeshore by pushing long poles into the lake bottom. The Coast Miwok and Costanoan tribes often traveled in tule rafts around the small bays, inlets, and shoreline of what is now called San Francisco Bay.

The Chumash were the only seagoing tribe. They were accomplished boat builders, making sturdy canoes of wooden planks, fastened together with animal hide ropes. The ropes were made waterproof with asphaltum from oil seeps in the Santa Barbara Channel. A crew of Chumash canoists using two-headed paddles could move swiftly even through the choppy coastal waters of the Pacific.

From their boats, Indians caught fish from the ocean with nets and spears and used harpoons to catch such sea mammals as otter, sea lion, and harbor seal. Harpoons were made from long, slender pieces of wood tipped with bone or antler barbs. Harpoons made to be thrown had a long string attached, made of animal hide, to retrieve them.

Another important source of food was large and small game. Deer, pronghorn antelope, mountain sheep, and elk were plentiful, as were rabbits, squirrels, raccoons, porcupines, small rodents, ducks and geese, quails, and songbirds. Hunters killed these animals using a variety of means—bows and arrows, nets, and snares. A stalking hunter often used an animal disguise—a set of deer antlers, the skinned head of an antelope, or an animal hide—so that he could approach animals without alerting them. Going along silently on all fours, he could get within shooting distance.

Sometimes game was driven past hunters lying in wait, or into corrals made of brush. Hunters hid behind boulders piled along known deer paths, or dug pits and covered them with tree boughs into which the deer fell. Hunters actually attracted bighorn rams to them by banging rocks together to mimic the sound of the rams fighting with their horns. This technique attracted curious bighorns, which were then killed.

Bows were made of various materials, depending on the locale. Bows and arrows made of reed, which grew along streams, were common in the south. In the north, wood from the yew tree was considered to be the finest material for a bow, as it was strong but supple. The bow was often reinforced with sinews to allow it to be pulled harder. The tip of a wooden arrow was ei-

▲ This wooden bow with painted decoration was made by a Hupa; it is nearly three feet long. The string is made of twisted animal sinew.

ther sharpened to a point, or a stone head was lashed to it. The head was often obsidian, a dark volcanic glass that is strong but can be flaked with a rock to create a point.

The meat of an animal was roasted in a fire, spitted on a piece of green wood (which was less likely to burn), slow-cooked over smoke, or dried in the sun.

A wide variety of plants was available throughout California. In marshes, Indians dug for arroweed roots; in the desert, they dug for the the onionlike bulbs of the desert lily. These tubers were baked or roasted, as we do potatoes. Women gathered the fresh young shoots of wild clover and wild onion as soon as they came up in spring. Strawberries, gooseberries, elderberries, and wild grapes were gathered in their season. The Costanoan turned manzanita berries into cider. The Luiseno gathered mushrooms, tree fungi, and a plant called lamb's-quarters. Seeds and nuts were important foods for all tribes. The chia plant produced a rich and oily seed. Women used woven beaters to shake chia seeds from the

▲ Made of fur and beautifully decorated with shell and feathers, these Karok quivers were used for carrying arrows.

plants into a flat basket, then dried the seeds and ground them into flour. A beverage was made by steeping the seeds in water. Desert dwellers utilized clarkia seeds, juniper and manzanita berries, and jojoba nuts. In arid regions where there were no oak trees, Indians ate the sweet and nutritious nut meats of the pinyon tree. The pine cones were shaken down and then roasted to release the pine nuts tucked inside.

In desert areas, pods from the honey mesquite bush were a favored food. In summer, women of the Cahuilla, Mojave, and Yuma tribes gathered the drooping pods, which are sweet and pulpy. The pods were dried, ground in wooden mortars, then soaked in earthware pots. The sticky and sweet mixture was sometimes made into balls as a kind of trail mix. The blossoms from the honey mesquite were soaked for several days to make a thirst-quenching drink. In the Mojave Desert, the joshua tree offered both seeds and flowers.

Fruit from the prickly pear, saguaro, and yucca also provided sustenance for desert dwellers. The tender young growth of the agave—including the stalk, leaves, and heart—was gathered in the spring and roasted for several days over a fire. The result, which was something like dried fruit, was sweet and kept well. Agave blossoms were boiled or dried to be eaten later.

Wherever there was water in desert places, wild plums and apricots could also be found. The Indians didn't eat the pulp of the plum but dried the fruit and extracted the kernels inside the pits. The fruit of the fan palm, eaten either fresh or dried, was a staple for the Indians living in the Anza-Borrego Desert. The small, dark blue dates hung in ripe clusters from the tall palms and were harvested by throwing a rope over them and pulling them down.

In addition to using plants for eating, most Indians had a basic knowledge of medicinal trees and herbs. There were also herb doctors and older women in the tribe who had specialized skills in the use of plants for healing.

For example, mistletoe berries were pounded and mixed with water; the resulting paste was applied to ease eye infections. The Miwok treated poison ivy with moss growing in Borax Lake. A mixture of angelica and tree bark was applied to relieve aches and pains. Branches of the California laurel were hung in a house to keep away fleas. Elderberry was used to make a splint for a broken bone.

The bark, roots, or leaves of a plant were often made into hot teas to relieve aches and pains and colds. Alder bark tea was used for stomach aches, willow bark tea for backache, spice bush bark tea for colds, and creosote leaf tea for colds and stomach cramps.

Sage was an important herb for Indians of the Anza-Borrego Desert. Believed to have powerful purifying abilities, sage was eaten, smoked, rubbed on the body in the sweathouse, and made into a tea. It was an essential part of mourning ceremonies and boys' and girls' initiation rites. Indians burned it on the cremation pyre because the fragrant smoke was said to ease grief.

Insects were an important source of protein for inhabitants of desert areas where game was scarce. Insects were eaten raw, or more commonly, boiled or roasted. Dried insect food kept well for leaner winter months. Ants, grasshoppers, caterpillers, and crickets were eaten as were the larvae of bees, moths, and yellowjackets. The

▲ Trays and plates were made using basketry techniques. This example was made by a member of the Tulare group.

Pomo dug for earthworms. Great Basin Indians depended on *kutsavi*, the larvae of flies that bred near the shores of Mono Lake. The dried kutsavi could be stored for long periods and cooked or eaten later.

Although most Indian groups simply gathered what nature had to offer, some practiced forms of land management to encourage better supplies of food. The Cahuilla cut back mesquite bushes to increase growth and the Ipai transplanted plants to form wild gardens that could be tended and harvested more effectively. Some Indians used controlled burning of grasslands and woodlands to promote fresh growth, which attracted browsing animals and provided open spaces where animals could be more easily hunted. Setting fires also reduced the possibility of destructive, out-of-control wildfires.

A number of tribes, such as the Hupa, Yurok, Cahuilla, Wintu, Maidu, Miwok, and Yokut, engaged in agriculture by cultivating the wild tobacco plant. Planting areas were chosen and burned off, and seeds gathered from the wild tobacco were planted in the rich ashes. The plots were regularly thinned and weeded. After drying, the leaves were smoked in clay pipes or wooden pipes with stone bowls. Since the major effect of the species of tobacco found in

California was sleepiness, it was usually smoked in small quantities mostly before going to bed. Generally, only men smoked tobacco. It was also smoked by the shamans during healing and used therapeutically as a painkiller.

The only true Indian farming culture in California was found along the banks of the Colorado River and in parts of the Imperial Valley. Tribes like the River Yuma procured about half their food supply from agriculture. The Colorado River floods once a year at the start of the growing season, depositing rich river mud on the bottomlands. The Colorado is so filled with silt that early white settlers said the water was "too thick to drink and too thin to plow." In this soil, the Indians planted five varieties of maize, three kinds of beans, and pumpkins. The Spanish brought with them watermelon and cowpea seeds, which the Indians also planted.

Of the nonfood resources the Indians utilized, wood was the most abundant. Oaks covered the lower foothills while mixed groves of pine and fir grew on the upper mountain slopes. Cottonwood, alder, and willow flourished along river bottoms. Wood was used for cooking utensils, houses, boats, and furniture such as low stools and was essential to the process of making fire. For example, the Wintu made fire by piling tinder of dry grass and dry, decayed pine into a boat-shaped piece of hard cedar. The fire maker then took a stick of soft wood like buckeye and twirled it between his or her palms. After a few minutes, the friction between the hard and soft wood created a spark and set the tinder on fire.

Plant fibers were another important resource. These were stripped from the leaves, stems, and roots of such plants as hemp, milkweed, agave, and Mojave yucca. These were woven into string, rope, net carrying bags, and woven sleeping mats. For fishing nets, northwestern tribes used the shoots of the ground iris. In the south, yucca fiber was used to make open sandals, which protected the feet against the desert's burning sands and rough rocks.

Throughout northern and central California, baskets woven from plant fiber were used for cooking, eating, and storage. For the basket frame, the strong, flexible boughs of the willow were preferred. Other materials used were bear grass, redbud, deer grass, the common cattail, and tule, another kind of cattail. Cooking baskets were made watertight by expert weaving and by adding pine tar or asphaltum to the seams. Basket fibers could be colored red, yellow, and black

▲ The Pomo were especially famous for their beautiful baskets. The basket here is adorned with feathers and shells.

using plant dyes from blackberries, sunflowers, buttercups, elderberries, and the indigo bush.

Many of the Indian baskets were beautiful as well as useful. Pomo women, for example, became famous for their tightly woven, decorated baskets, which used small shells, porcupine quills, and feathers for decorations. The women wove into the baskets brightly colored feathers from the acorn and pileated woodpeckers, the California quail, the red-winged blackbird, and the mallard duck. Pomo baskets were much-prized items of trade.

A variety of materials, including wood, bone, shell, horn, and stone were used for cooking and eating utensils such as soapstone griddles, spoons carved from elkhorn, and wooden stirring spoons. The holes in abalone shells were sealed with asphalt and the shells used for bowls and spoons. Grinding stones made from hard wood,

LANGUAGES OF CALIFORNIA

About 60 separate languages and more than 100 dialects were spoken by the Indians of California. For the sake of simplicity, the languages can be divided into five family groups. The chart below lists the main language families and some of the tribes that spoke them.

ALGONQUIAN FAMILY
Yurok

ATHAPASCAN FAMILY
Hupa

HOKAN FAMILY
Chumash
Pomo
Yahi

PENUTIAN FAMILY
Maidu
Miwok
Patwin
Wintun
Yokut

UTO-AZTECAN FAMILY
Cahuilla
Cupeno
Diegueno
Gabrielino
Luiseno
Serrano

▲ The techniques of basket weaving were also applied to clothing, as shown by this Karok basketry skirt.

sandstone, or basalt were used to grind nuts and seeds. The tribes of the Santa Barbara Channel made cooking pots by carving out pieces of soft soapstone.

Tools included needles and awls (pointed tools for making holes) made from mammal bones or horns such as deer antlers. Wedges carved from elkhorn and whalebone were used to pry shellfish off tidal rocks and to open them. Mussel shells were made into adzes. Desert dwellers used the hooked spines of the barrel cactus as sewing awls.

For personal adornment—for example, to decorate hair or make necklaces and earrings—shells, pelican bones, small stones, and feathers

◄ A Tolowa woman from northern California wears a traditional outfit around 1890. Her hat and skirt use basketry weaving, and she wears a buckskin dance apron decorated with shells. She is also wearing necklaces of shell beads. Thimbles are attached to the ends of her hair ornaments; these will make a tinkling noise when she dances.

▲ Buckskin was a common material for clothing. This Hupa buckskin dress is decorated with fringe and beads made of shells.

▲ These Maidu earrings are made from feathers, shell beads, pieces of abalone shell, and bird bones.

were used. Plant dyes were used for tattoos, a practice common in the north, or to paint faces for ceremonies. For clothing, women wore a two-piece short skirt of fringed leather or woven from grass, rush, or shredded cottonwood or willow bark. For most of the year, Indian men wore nothing but soft animal hide moccasins, sometimes made with a tougher rawhide sole. In winter or bad weather, men and women wore a robe or blanket of rabbit, wildcat, or deer skins. Along the coast, sea otter was prized for its softness, warmth, and ability to shed rain and snow. Snowshoes were fashioned from animal skins and leather thongs. Hides were prepared by soaking the skins in water, then stretching them tight with wooden pegs and scraping the inside with a pumice stone until the skin was soft.

A contemporary visitor to the Santa Barbara coastline will see the oil rigs out in the bay, bringing up petroleum. The coast-dwelling Indians were the first to discover this resource. They found small seeps of asphaltum floating on the ocean surface, pushed up from the ocean floor.

Asphaltum, a thick, brown or black tarry substance, is a natural by-product of petroleum. The Indians used it as a glue to mend broken tools and attach knife blades and arrowheads to their shafts and as a sealant for baskets, boats, and eating vessels,

Clearly, California Indians lived according to the rule, "Waste not, want not." The land was the source of their life and Indians believed it should be treated with respect and care. They viewed human life and the environment as interconnected, and therefore saw their role in the world as one of cooperation, not conquest. Before an Indian went out to hunt, he gave thanks to the deer. A hunter who failed to come home with game might say, "The deer don't want to die for me today." The practical result of this philosophy was that the Indians didn't use up or waste their natural resources. They didn't overfish the waters and when they gathered food, they took what they needed and left the rest. In this way, they could continue to take advantage of the bounty of nature.

LIVING ON THE LAND

THE REGION

▼ The Grapevine Mountains rise over the dunes of Death Valley. Some California Indians managed to thrive even in this arid wasteland.

◀ Tule reeds, also known as cattails, grow abundantly along the marshy areas of California. Tule was widely used by the Native Americans of the region to make shelters, boats, and more.

◀ The towering redwood trees and moist climate of northern California are a sharp contrast to Death Valley. The Native Americans of California are as diverse as the geography of the region.

▼ This rugged coastline is near Point Reyes north of San Francisco. It was part of the homelands of the Coast Miwok tribe.

▶ Land mammals such as deer, rabbits, and elk were hunted with bows and arrows. Elk still roam protected areas of California.

◀ California's long seacoast provided a bounty of fish and sea mammals to the Native Americans. Sea lions and seals were hunted for their meat and fur.

▼ The plentiful waterfowl in California provided food as well as feathers for ceremonial headdresses and costumes. Waterfowl were caught by throwing nets over resting birds or by raising a net across a known flyway.

HUNTING FOR FOOD

FOODS FROM THE EARTH

◀ Some tribes made cider from berries from the manzanita bush. Here, water is being poured over the crushed berries.

▶ Acorns from seven varieties of oak trees were an **essential** part of the diet for most California Indians. This is a tanbark oak tree.

▼ The fruit of the desert palm tree was eaten by southern California Indians. The dried dates were also used as a trade item with other tribes.

▲ The flowers and fruits of the joshua tree were used for food by desert-dwelling Indians.

CHAPTER TWO

LIVING

The world of the California Indians centered on the family and small communities or villages. Describing California Indians, anthropologists define "tribe" as a group of people who spoke the same language, not as a cohesive political or social unit. For example, the Hupa tribe consisted of 12 separate settlements strung out along both sides of the Trinity River, all speaking a form of the Hupa language. But this language group—that is, tribe—wasn't governed by one chief or one set of laws and those living in the individual villages felt their allegiance to their village, not to other settlements that spoke the same language.

Some villages were small, consisting of extended families of about 50 people. Others were settlements of several hundred people, while still others were large enough—from 1,000 to 2,000 people—to be called a town. A village was loosely governed by a chief, always a man, assisted by his council, older men who were often relatives of the chief. A chief often had a trusted assistant who acted as a moderator between him and the tribe. The shaman, or sacred doctor, and members of the secret religious societies might also be members of the council. In fact, in many villages, membership in a religious society was a prerequisite to obtaining political power. (More information about religious systems can be found in the next chapter.)

Many became leaders by virtue of being the wealthiest men in their villages. If chiefs weren't wealthy when they took the office, they usually acquired wealth soon after from gifts and political favors—for example, in bigger villages they weren't required to work and were given food, lavish clothing, and large homes. However, leadership qualities were also important and if a chief lacked them, he might be out of a job. A Yuma Indian described a good chief in this way:

> You know how some men are quick and strong and know the things to do, how people like to do things for them, and how they have a gift for getting everybody cheerful? Well, those men were *kwoxot*—tribal leaders.

A chief's main duties were managerial. In smaller villages, chiefs gave advice, provided moral support, and settled small disputes. In larger groups, the chief's responsibilities might include arranging for ceremonies and dances, entertaining visitors, organizing large hunting expeditions, and supervising the construction of communal buildings.

▲ Obsidian, or volcanic glass, is strong but flakes easily into sharp edges. It's favored for arrowheads.

In the northwest, true chiefs were lacking. Northwest Indians were highly concerned with social status, which they defined by material wealth—animal skins, obsidian knives, and the currency of exchange, which was ropes of shells. The emphasis on individual wealth elevated family money and power over community values. The fundamental social unit was the family, not the village; therefore the highest leadership position was headman of a large and wealthy family. The headman usually had a large number of relatives and hangers-on around him; he was influential in his village but didn't have absolute political power to make decisions regarding the village as a whole. If a crime occurred—say, murder or theft—then an independent mediator was hired to negotiate an agreement between the two parties. Money, not punishment, was the preferred compensation.

Few permanent military leaders developed among California Indians because war wasn't a frequent occurence, but leaders with special skills or bravery arose from time to time to direct a war party. Among the California Indians, war was primarily defensive rather than aggressive. Tribes didn't go to war to conquer new territories, acquire wealth, or control new populations. Most wars took place between villages over disagreements concerning territorial rights to oak groves or hunting and fishing lands. Other reasons for going to war included theft, insulting a member of the tribe, kidnapping women, and murder.

If war was deemed necessary by the elders of the tribe, the most popularly used military tactic was ambush or surprise attack. The weapons were usually hunting weapons—bows and arrows, spears, and clubs. The Maidu warriors covered their bodies with elk hide or an armor of hard wooden sticks as protection against the poisoned arrows of their enemies. The warriors were led into battle by the chief or the warrior in charge and were followed by women and children who carried supplies and helped out in the battle by retrieving the enemy's arrows. Conflicts could be short but devastating, wiping out entire villages in a single raid. Male prisoners of war were slain, while female prisoners were taken hostage.

Sometimes a formal confrontation was arranged in lieu of a bloody battle. The two sides met at an appointed time, threw rocks and stones at each other, and hurled insults. Few casualties, if any, resulted, and the two chiefs usually negotiated a peace and organized a conciliatory dance between the opposing sides.

In the northeast, Indians were subject to attack from the north by Klamath Indians who often took hostages, which they sold or traded as slaves on the Columbia River in Oregon. In the south, the Yuma and the Mojave tribes often went to war and would sometimes travel for a week or more to reach an enemy tribe. A class of warriors was specially trained and armed with mesquite-wood clubs as well as bows and arrows. If victorious they took both scalps and captives.

Relations between many villages and tribes were friendly, however. Marrying between villages was common and increased communication and trade between the groups. Sometimes several villages joined forces on a seasonal basis to work together—for example, to catch salmon during the spawning runs. Hupa villages built communal fish weirs and the Pomo groups linked up along the Russian River to control their section of the river and protect their fishing rights. Neighboring villages often got together to participate in

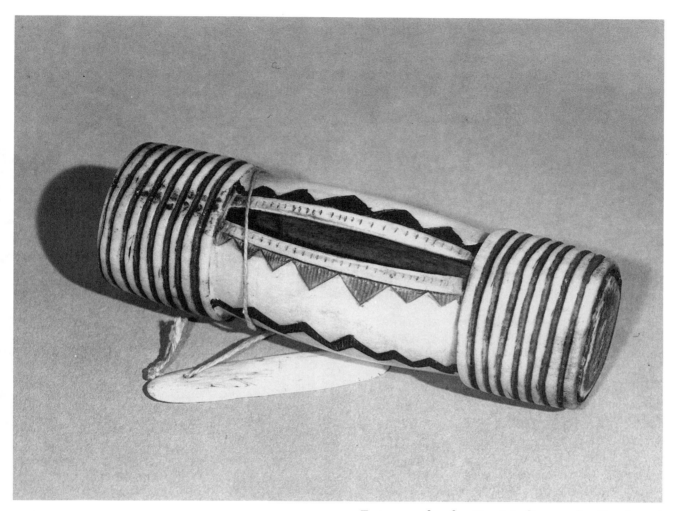

▲ The California Indians used a form of money made from shells. This elkhorn purse was used by a Hupa to hold the shells.

large-scale ceremonial festivities and religious systems, such as the World Renewal Cult, which included many villages and tribes. A well-developed trail system existed throughout California, used not only for a group's seasonal migrations but to visit neighboring tribes.

TRADE

Tribes connected to each other through trade. Trading missions were usually undertaken by heads of households or by traders who made regularly scheduled trips. Through trade, Indians could widen and increase their food supply and survive in times of scarcity. One tribe might trade acorns or obsidian for dried fish—or whatever was a scarce commodity in its territory.

For example, the Kami Indians, who lived west of the Colorado River, traded watermelons to the Diegueno Indians in exchange for acorns, which weren't available in their region. Other desert groups traded mesquite pods and palm fruit for acorns, or acquired harvesting rights in neighboring foothills. The Atsugewi and the Achomawi bought salt from the Yana who, in turn, were allowed to fish and gather acorns from their neighbors' land.

Trading also increased the supply of desirable goods. For example, Chumash tribes traded among themselves such items as shell jewelry, animal skins, deer antlers, knives, bows and arrows, baskets, and food delicacies such as wild cherry or chia seed. From the Mojave, the Chumash acquired clay pottery and red dye and from the Yokut, black pigment, melons, tobacco, herbs, and salt.

In addition to barter, goods could be bought and sold using a currency of exchange. Currency was primarily based on shells. "Money" shells

were produced by boring holes in clam or dentalium shells, stringing them like beads on fiber or leather thongs, then rounding and polishing them by rolling on sandstone. Larger clams were broken up into smaller pieces. The trading value of the beads was determined in different ways. In the south, the measure was the width of a man's hand, while Indians like the Pomo and Maidu of central California counted the number of beads. In addition to shell-bead money, obsidian, magnesite, and baskets were also highly valued and used in trade. The tribe receiving the currency could use it at a future time when it was in need or could keep it as valuables or displays of wealth.

Some villages hosted large "trade feasts," especially if they had a surplus of a specific commodity, like fish. These events were attended by men from many different villages who socialized during the trade feast by getting together in the host's sweathouse, gambling, smoking, and swapping stories. After several days, the traders exchanged goods or money—say, magnesite beads for fish.

FINDING FOOD

Although the whole village often got together to fish or hunt, finding food was the responsibility of individual families. Women taught the girls the skills they needed and men taught the boys. However, this division wasn't rigid. Men sometimes helped the women gather acorns and women often fished and caught small game. If a woman was widowed, she might engage in "men's work" in order to supply her family.

In larger villages, which were like small towns, some work activities became specialized. Among the Pomo and Chumash, for example, there were professional positions for those who hunted and fished, made bead strings, and crafted bows, arrows, nets, and baskets. The specialists traded their skills or goods for food or other necessities.

▶ A Diegueno village around 1905 is shown here. Some of the buildings are made in the traditional way, but a plank house has also been built.

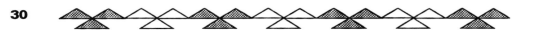

MARRIAGE AND FAMILIES

Potential suitors in marriage were often evaluated in terms of their ability to be good providers. During courtship, a man or a man's family might bring small gifts like animal skins, feathers, or food, which would show the woman's family he possessed hunting and fishing prowess. Marriages were usually arranged by the parents of a young man and woman who had reached puberty. A woman could refuse a suitor although she couldn't marry against her parents' wishes. Since individuals couldn't marry their near relatives, men often had to go courting in neighboring villages. Social status could be important in assessing a suitor, and a poor suitor might be discouraged by a large and wealthy family who wanted to form an alliance with another well-to-do family.

In some cultures, the marriage ceremony was elaborate but most often it was a simple matter of the couple moving in together, accompanied by an exchange of gifts and a celebration dinner. Divorce in Indian culture was just as informal, though it was easier for men to divorce than for women. Common reasons for divorce included infidelity and sterility, and for women, cruelty and abuse.

Polygynous families—that is, marriages with more than one wife—were not uncommon among chiefs, religious leaders, and wealthy men. Having more than one wife was advantageous to men for economic reasons. Since the processing of plant food, which was a woman's job, required intensive labor, more women in a household meant more material wealth. To women, polygynous marriages offered the protection of family life in situations where there were fewer men than women. A polygynous marriage commonly involved two sisters who knew each other and were more liable to get along well.

Among northwestern groups, a man purchased his bride from her family with money, furs, and valuable feathers. Female children, therefore, were prized more than male ones since they represented potential wealth. Some poor men promised their infant daughters in marriage in order to obtain the bride price in advance.

A newly married couple might live with either of their in-law families if their relatives had room or needed some more helping hands. The family group might include a grandmother and a grandfather, younger sisters and brothers. However, men were forbidden to speak to their mothers-in-law and daughters-in-law. Direct address was also discouraged between women and their male in-laws. Some groups got around this taboo by using the more generalized, plural form—like the "you all" of the American South—when speaking to an in-law. After a year or so the couple might settle on their own and build their own family house. With time, this arrangement often grew into an extended family as relatives such as a widowed parent came to live there.

HOMES AND VILLAGES

Family houses were small dwellings where the family took shelter, cooked, ate, and slept during cold or rainy weather, and stored food, clothes, cooking utensils, hunting weapons, fur blankets, and personal items. On the fringes of the settlement there were work areas for butchering animals and cutting wood, granaries for storing acorns, and a cemetery.

Construction of family houses varied with locale. Northern tribes made rectangular houses from cedar or redwood planks with a narrow hole in one wall to serve as a door. The floor of the house was packed dirt with a fire pit in the center, bordered with stones and encircled with a wooden platform where the family slept and kept their possessions. Sometimes a brush fence was built a few feet from the house and acorns were dried in the space between. The Hupa cobbled the area in front of their houses with small stones.

Further south, Indians built houses of wooden frames, which they covered with various materials. The Yana built a cone-shaped family house with tall poles, about 20 feet in diameter and 10 feet tall at the center pole. They covered the poles with slabs of pine or cedar bark, adding earth along the base for better insulation. A hole in the middle of the roof let in light and let out smoke from the fire. When it rained, an animal skin could be used to cover the smokehole. Among the Maidu, this frame construction was partially submerged and covered with earth, resulting in well-insulated earth-covered lodgehouses. The Miwok hung a grass mat at the door opening.

▶ The Chumash lived in homes made of grass thatch over a wooden frame. In this picture, taken in the 1920s, the frame is clearly shown.

▲ This family of California Indians is shown outside its home around 1886. The frame of the dwelling is covered with reed mats.

Other tribes covered the frames with lightweight plants such as cattails, grass, arrowweed, rush, or tule. These materials were bunched together and laid down like shingles. Along the coast, the Chumash built circular house frames of willow poles, which they thatched with tule. The Spaniard Longino Martinez described a Chumash village in 1792:

> These Indians . . . arrange their houses in groups. The houses are well constructed, round like an oven, spacious and fairly comfortable; light enters from a hole in the roof. Their beds are made on frames and they cover themselves with skins and shawls. The beds have divisions between them like the cabins of a ship, so that if many people sleep in one house, they do not see one another. In the middle of the floor they make a fire for cooking seeds, fish, and other foods. . . .

In summer months, families slept under the stars or put up simple frames, which they covered with oak boughs to let in the breezes. When families migrated to harvest fruits and seeds or to the oak groves for the acorn harvest, easy-to-build temporary dwellings were set up in camp.

In addition to a number of family houses, a village usually consisted of a somewhat larger chief's house, a dance house or assembly building for large gatherings, and a sweathouse. Some dance houses or assembly buildings were larger versions of family dwellings. The Western Pomo built an assembly house about 70 feet across as well as a special earth-covered building for religious ceremonies. The Costanoan built a thatched assembly house large enough for 200 villagers and an enclosure for dances made by putting up a circular brush fence. Both the assembly house and the "dance plaza" were in the center of the village. Some tribes had no formal structures for dances or religious observances; others, like the Yokut, put up a temporary ramada, or shelter, during mourning ceremonies.

One of the most important and widely used structures in many California Indian villages was the sweathouse. The sweathouse was used primarily by males, although females sometimes visited during special occasions. The sweathouse was an important social institution. Men used the sweathouse building as a kind of men's club, where they could get together, talk, smoke, and relax. They sometimes slept there, and in some

▲ This Costanoan sweathouse is a modern reconstruction, made from tule and cattail reeds. Note the opening in the roof to let out smoke.

tribes, the entire adult male population lived there, returning to the family house only for meals.

Used as a sauna, the sweathouse was believed to promote cleanliness, health, and well-being; to cure illness; and perhaps to remove the human smell before hunts. A fire was built and after spending some time in the hot confines of the sweathouse, those inside would leave and plunge into nearby cold streams.

The chief characteristic of all sweathouses was, of course, the central firepit, usually lined with stones. A typical sweathouse, such as the one built by the Coast Miwok, was a circular structure sunk in the ground about five feet. It was of frame construction, covered with brush and grass, then plastered with earth.

Women also had a retreat from family life when they visited a small lean-to during their monthly menstruation period. Some Indian tribes viewed menstruation as having harmful properties, while such tribes as the Yurok believed that a woman was full of spiritual energy during menstruation. A Yurok woman spent that time meditating, bathing, and performing certain rituals, using her seclusion to gather her spiritual powers.

CHILDREN

The birth of a child was attended with great care. During pregnancy and when children were born, both the mother and father engaged in activities designed to encourage the health of the infant. When the mother went into labor, she retired to

the menstrual dwelling, accompanied by her mother and sisters and a midwife. The father often went up into the hills to pray for the child and gather firewood to make a warming blaze for the mother and child. After birth, stones were warmed in the fire and then placed on the mother's abdomen to ease the pain. The mother's female kinfolk took care of the newborn for a few weeks to give the mother time to rest and recuperate. In some tribes, the father was forbidden to hunt, fish, or smoke during this time. Probably this taboo was in place to keep the new father at home with his wife and child.

Children were given a great deal of attention and love, cared for not only by their parents but by grandparents, aunts, uncles, and older siblings. Mothers often carried their infants in cradleboards on their backs when they went acorn gathering. When mothers were too busy, fathers took on the job of caring for and playing with the younger children. Indian children received love and care, but they were also strictly trained in how to behave. Disobedience, lying, and fighting were punished by whipping with a willow switch.

Until children reached puberty, they were not expected to do real work. When female children followed their mothers on gathering expeditions, it was not to pitch in to gather food, but because mothers wanted to watch over them. Indian children had plenty of time to play. Girls played a game in which they held hands and danced around a ring. They held jumping contests and, if they lived near mountains, they might go on climbing expeditions. They gathered wild birds' eggs, made dolls of tule rush, and built dolls' houses of mud. Among the Modoc, boys played hide and seek and dodgeball; they swam, raced, and wrestled; they made bows of young juniper boughs. However, children did often practice or play at such skills as basket making and bow and arrow craft, much as children today play house or play with toy cars or learn to cook. For example, boys might practice with slingshots, or go out hunting chipmunks, rabbits, and frogs (though they didn't necessarily eat what they killed). One Indian remembered: "My parents were proud of me; and the prouder they were of me the more I wanted to work hard and the better I felt. So I was never lazy."

TRADITIONAL MUSIC

Being a good singer was an important accomplishment for California Indians. These two Cahuilla women were photographed while singing in 1903.

▲ When a young girl reached puberty, a dance was held to celebrate. This photo of Diegueno women was taken in 1931 at such a dance.

As girls and boys grew closer to puberty, they were trained to assume their prospective roles as women and men. A girl's coming of age was an important event, marked by special intitiation rites. At the time of a girl's first menstruation, she underwent a period of special instruction and celebration, which lasted between two and 10 days. During this, she was usually isolated in the menstrual building and instructed in her future role as a wife. A set of taboos strictly limited her diet and activities; for example, she might be forbidden to eat salt or meat or drink water. She might be asked to leave the hut to perform a woman's tasks such as gathering firewood. When she emerged from her isolation, a celebration dance was held and the girl was given special presents.

Among southern tribes, the girls' initiation rites included ritualistic "roasting." The girl was placed face down in a pit of sand for three nights and four days. It was believed that this would make the girl strong enough to bear children and to endure hardships. She was attended by older women in the tribe, who sang to her and gave her instructions on her future life as an adult woman.

After the ritual roasting, the girl was shown an image drawn in colored sand on the ground. The sand painting, also used in the boys' initiation rites, was used to instruct the girl in her place—and her tribe's—in the universe. Using different kinds of colored earth mixed with sand, the sand painter drew familiar landmarks such as the local mountains, star systems like the Milky Way and the Pleiades, the sun and the moon and the sky, and figures from mythology.

Boys' initiation rites were less elaborate or even nonexistent, sometimes only consisting of a gift of the first adult bow and arrow. However, at adolesence, many boys were initiated into secret religious societies. (More information about these societies can be found in the following chapter about religion.)

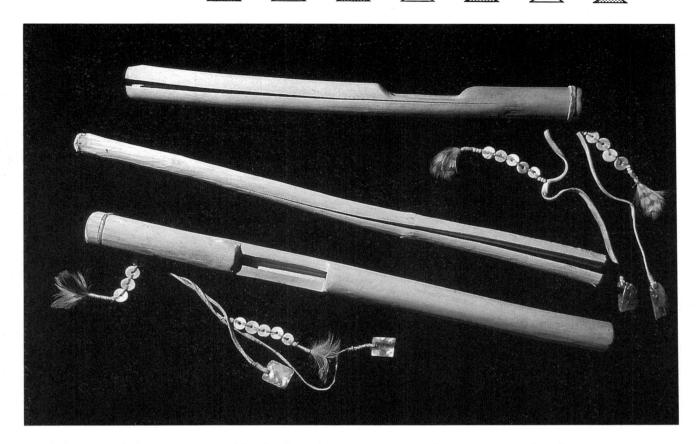

▲ Elderberry wood clappers were used by the Central Miwok in their dances.

CEREMONIES AND DANCES

In addition to girls' and boys' initiation rites, a tribe might organize more than a dozen dances, or rituals, during the year: shaman dances, mourning dances, harvest feasts, and sacred dances, as well as dozens of smaller informal dancing events to bring luck in hunting or give thanks for it. These dances were religious in the sense that they offered up thanks and gave prayers to a higher power. They were also occasions for celebration, like the many "first-fruit" ceremonies, which celebrated food harvests. Most important among these were the Salmon Dance in the spring and the Acorn Feast in the fall. The salmon or acorns were cooked by a ceremonial leader, who said prayers and repeated magic formulas. Then the people engaged in feasting, singing, and dancing. The Pomo had ceremonies for the arrival of clover, manzanita berries, and wild strawberries. The Hupa celebrated catching the first eel in the spring.

In the Coast Miwok tribe, a woman was responsible for organizing several of the dances, including the Acorn Dance, arranging for the food, the invitations, and the dancers. This woman was in charge of construction whenever a new dance house was to be built. She had an assistant who was in charge of the woman's dance house.

Summer or fall food harvests were an occasion for large parties and celebrations, some of which could last a week or longer. If a village had an abundance of food, it held a kind of open house for those living in nearby villages. There was singing, dancing, plenty of food, and gambling. Gambling was a popular sport throughout most of California. One of the most popular adult games involving gambling was the grass game. Both men and women played this game in which a player hid a pair of sticks or duck bones in their hands, concealed by a bundle of grass; another player guessed which hand held the sticks or bones. Wagers were placed using shell currency or magnesite. In one game of chance, women played dice using dice made from walnut or snail shells, filled with asphaltum to make them heavy. Bets were taken against whether the dice would land on the flat or curved side of the

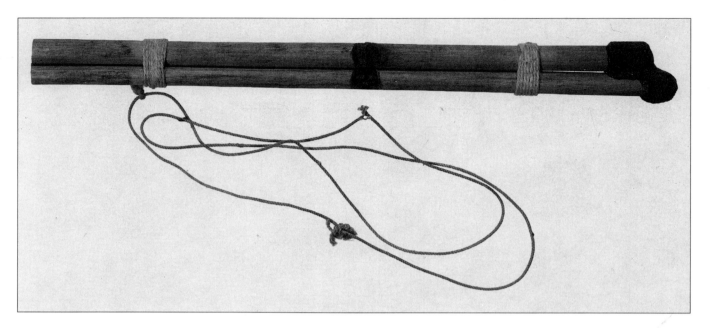

shell. Indians used various techniques to improve their betting luck, including fasting, visiting a shaman, and ingesting datura, or jimsonweed.

At sporting events, men and women could show off their physical strength and skills. Jumping and wrestling contests, races, pitching rocks, and archery contests were all common. Shinny, a form of field hockey, and football or soccer, were played separately by men and women. The results of athletic events were often wagered on.

Music was an important part of California Indian life. Most music was provided by the human voice, so good singers and good songs were prized. A favorite accompaniment was the rattle, often made from turtle shells, gourds, pottery, or bundles of deer hoofs. A common rattle was made by filling emptied, dried insect cocoons with pebbles, seeds, or small shells and attached them to handles of bird quills, wood, or bone. "Clappers" were sticks split halfway down the middle so that the two halves clapped or rattled together.

Whistles were made from the hollow bones of large birds, from elk, deer, or rodent bones, and from hollowed-out pieces of wood. "Foot-drums"—large hollowed-out logs placed over a pit and stomped rhythmically—and other drums were important in ceremonial dances. The "bull-roarer" was made with a leather thong attached to the end of a thin, flat piece of wood. When swung rapidly, the wood gave off a fierce humming noise, like a roaring bull.

▲ A Pomo made this double flute. The two tubes are closed at the end and held together by asphaltum, a type of tar formed when oil seeps naturally into the ocean.

Elderberry provided wood for flutes, much used by suitors during courtship. Both men and women sang love songs. Here is a song composed by a suitor rejected because he was too poor. He imagines that his beloved becomes as poor as a bear who is reduced to foraging for clover:

Down in the west lying down,
Down in the west lying down,
A beautiful bear I found
Tearing up clover in fistfuls.

Many songs belonged to the religious ceremonies but many were sung just for pleasure, or to express grief or joy. The following was sung by the Maidu to increase the harvest:

The acorns come down from heaven.
I plant the short acorns in the valley.
I plant the long acorns in the valley.
I sprout, I, the black acorn, sprout, I sprout.

STORIES AND RECREATION

Storytelling was another popular form of recreation. On winter evenings, men, women, and children gathered around a blazing fire, in the sweathouse or in one of the communal dwellings, to hear stories told. Here was a rich body of ancient literature—stories, myths, and

tainment to while away the long winter nights.

Some stories described historical events, such as warfare. Many described deities or pictured heroes who had magical or godlike properties. For example, the Hupa hero Lost-across-the-ocean was said to have freed the salmon who were imprisoned by an old woman. The Cupeno hero Avenger won a fight by using a bearskin that magically turned into a real and ferocious bear.

Many of the stories were creation stories or explanations of how things came to be: why acorns are bitter, how the mountains were made, where fire came from, or how the constellations came into being. One central California creation story explained that a deity called "One-who-is-above" made the world out of formless water and mud; another described two quarreling brothers who come up out of the sea to make the world and everything in it; still another described Sky and Earth, a brother and sister who were the first parents of the world.

Animals were an important part of many stories. Stories explained how they acquired certain characteristics—for example, how the sea otter got its short arms or how the mouse got its white feet and tail. Animals were given human characteristics of envy or greed, courage or craftiness.

One of the most popular animal figures was the Coyote. He was pictured variously as a mischief maker, a foolish victim of his own pranks, and a near-deity who created many of the world's good things. The Pomo believed he brought light into the world and the Karok said that he put salmon into the Klamath River. In one Pomo story, Coyote helped a village during a great drought, when it had nothing to eat. Listening to the advice of the Great Spirit, Coyote began by gobbling up grasshoppers who were eating all the Indians' grass seed. Then he dug a spring in the center of a dry lake so that it filled with water. The Great Spirit congratulated Coyote on his unselfish acts and finished the job by turning the remaining grasshoppers into fish. In his role as a trickster, Coyote brought evil things into the world in order to cause mischief or to get things he selfishly wanted for himself.

Storytelling formed a kind of oral library of shared knowledge, preserving the history, values, and literature of the tribe. It was a communal experience and everyone—women, men, children, and old people—all gathered at the winter fires to hear how the Big Dipper was formed or about the clever pranks of Coyote.

▲ This Maidu rattle was made using an insect cocoon. It is decorated with feathers and shells and attached to a long wooden handle.

poems—not written down but spoken and remembered by generations of storytellers. The storyteller was usually an older man who knew tribal folklore and was skilled at acting. As he told the story, he pretended to be the characters described, acting out their gestures and dramatically portraying fear, joy, or mischievousness. Suspense and humor were important elements. Though most stories had a religious character or a moral point, storytelling was primarily enter-

▲ Made by a Hupa, this square drum has exactly the same design painted on both sides.

HOW THEY LIVED

ASPECTS OF DAILY LIFE

▲ Strings of clamshell beads were used for money. In this picture, the clamshell beads have been made into a lovely necklace.

▲ This bladelike tool is made from chert, a flintlike rock
that can be flaked to produce a razor-sharp edge.

▲ Acorns were placed in the holes worn into this rock slab and crushed with a pestle of wood or stone. The crushed acorns were then soaked in water to remove the bitter tannin.

BASKETS

▼ A gentle motion of the winnowing tray was used to separate the edible parts of seeds from the chaff.

▶ A porridge of ground acorns and water was a staple food. It was cooked in watertight baskets. Wooden tongs were used to pick up hot stones that were then dropped into the mixture to heat it.

▼ These Miwok baskets hold two acorn foods—on the left, a gelled biscuit and on the right, acorn soup.

HOMES

◀ The Yurok lived in northern California along the Klamath River. They built their houses from slabs or planks of wood.

◀ The Coastal Miwok made buildings such as these. The wooden frame is thatched with tule.

▼ Cedar was used to build this Sierra Miwok roundhouse, or assembly house. Cedar wood is strong and acts as a natural insect repellent.

▲ Slabs of redwood bark were used to make this Coastal Miwok house.

CHAPTER THREE

RELIGION AND BELIEFS

ost California Indians believed in a supreme being who had created the earth or who was in charge of it. They called this creator "He who walks alone," "Above Person," "Great Traveler," or the "Immortal One." The Cahto called him the Thunder God and the Maidu called him Earth Maker. For some Indians, the Creator was not a humanlike figure but an animal, often the golden eagle. The Creator could also be the coyote, hawk, condor, owl, fox, roadrunner, deer, hummingbird, or raven. Many Indians offered small prayers to the Creator throughout the day. They might pray upon rising or going to bed, while washing in the river in the morning, before eating, or when sick. Hunters prayed for success before going off on a hunting trip.

Indians believed that everything in the universe had a kind of spiritual power—animals and plants and mountains. A Nomlaki women told an interviewer in this century, "Everything in this world talks, just as we are [talking] now—the trees, rocks, everything. But we cannot understand them, just as the White people do not understand the Indians." There were many taboos and rituals designed to please the host of spirits found in the world. For example, someone passing by a mountain or rock formation might say a prayer to ensure safe passage through the landscape. The Shasta had special songs to bring hunting luck and ward off rattlesnakes and grizzly bears. The Miwok believed that disturbing a porcupine produced headache or rheumatism. To promote the health of her child, a pregnant woman wouldn't look at the sun or moon.

Like people everywhere, Indians tried to answer the questions: Where have we come from? Where are we going? Central California groups believed that the world began as a flood and land was formed when Turtle brought up a bit of ocean mud in his teeth. The Luiseno's explanation of creation stated that in the beginning, the world was nothingness. There were two beings, a brother and sister, called Empty and Vacant. Out of these two evolved Brother Sky and Sister Earth who married to produce all the things in the world. The Yurok had stories about "Widower across the ocean," who created many things in the world, and "Down-stream sharp," who killed monsters at the beginning of the world. A bearded dwarf, carrying acorns on his back, was the Yurok master of the plant world.

DEATH AND MOURNING

The Indians believed that, after death, a person's soul left the body. The Maidu called the soul the

▲ Plume sticks, decorated with beads and feathers, were carried in some dances. This plume stick was used by a Maidu in the late 19th century.

"heart" and when a person died they said, "His heart has gone away." Maidu believed that the soul of a good person traveled east along the Milky Way, toward the Creator. Good souls found themselves in heaven, where there was no work, only feasting and games and pleasure, while bad souls were condemned to an eternal reincarnation as bushes or rocks. The Yurok believed that the dead were ferried across an underground river to the afterlife. Rich men who had done much for the village by organizing dances would live in the sky, as would shamans and ceremonial leaders.

After death, souls stayed on earth and haunted the world of the living. A shooting star or a dust eddy was believed to be the soul of the dead. Indians did not see their dead ancestors as kind or helpful beings but as presences to be feared. Throughout all of California, Indians practiced one important taboo: It was forbidden to speak the names of the dead, since that was believed to attract them. The Hupa wore grass necklaces to ward off dreaming about the dead. The Yokut said this prayer to persuade souls to travel on to the next life:

> You are going to another land
> You will like that land
> You shall not stay here.

When a person died, he or she was often dressed in fine clothes, like otter skins, and either cremated or buried in cemeteries located close to the village. The Chumash marked grave sites with wooden poles and whalebones. The clothes and possessions of the deceased, along with gifts from relatives, like baskets, were buried or cremated with the body. Sometimes even houses were burned, especially if the person had been an important chief or shaman. Grieving relatives expressed mourning by cutting off their hair and smearing their faces and bodies with pine pitch, ashes, charcoal, or white clay. Women didn't wash their faces but merely waited for the pitch or clay to wear off.

Some tribes regularly held mourning ceremonies—once a year or once every four or five years—to honor and grieve for those who had died since the last ceremony. During the cere-

▶ Elaborate headdresses were worn by shamans when they performed dances. This Maidu headdress is made of feathers.

▲ Woven of milkweed fiber, this headdress was worn by a Karok shaman when performing in the Jumping Dance.

▲ Although the Mission Indians were converted to Catholicism, they did not give up their traditions. This Luiseno shaman is calling for rain in a photo taken in 1904.

mony, which lasted a week or so, the village sang, danced, and feasted, sometimes burning food and other gifts as an offering to the dead. The Yokut's Dance of the Dead began with a leader addressing the group:

> Make ready for the mourning. Let all make ready. Everybody make ready. Prepare your offerings. Your offerings to the dead. Have them all ready. Show them to the mourners. Let them see your sympathy. The mourning comes on. It hastens. Everybody make ready.

Another form of the mourning ceremony was the "ghost dance." During the ghost dance, male dancers impersonated the spirits of the dead. The ceremony began with the dancers lighting fires on the hills, then running back to the village and entering the dance house. For several days, the dancers acted out frightening actions, danced, smoked, ate, and used the sweathouse. During this time, the dancers spoke a special language, using opposites to refer to things. For example, they said "east" when they meant "west." The ghost dance ended with a large feast.

SHAMANS

One of the most important people in Indian spiritual life was the shaman, who combined the roles of doctor and priest. The shaman's specific job was to diagnose and cure illness but he or she also was a religious leader. Shamans were respected and prestigious members of their community, often serving as advisors to chiefs and other religious leaders. In some tribes, they had a wide range of responsibilities, such as predicting the weather or naming children.

Most importantly, the shaman provided a link between ordinary people and spiritual power. In his book on the Chumash, Bruce W. Miller describes the Indian view of spiritual power:

▲ In the Jumping Dance, participants wore headbands
made from the feathers of woodpeckers.

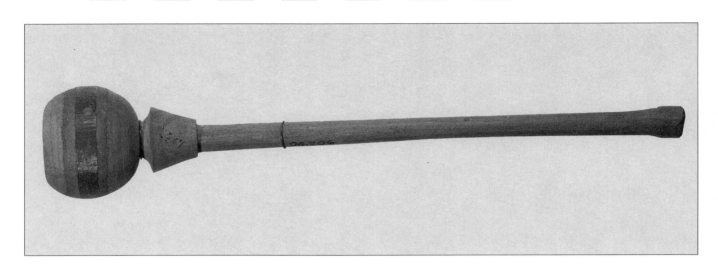

"Power was neutral. . . . It could be used for both good and bad purposes. It was the user of that power and the path taken that gave power its positive and negative aspects." The shaman was able, because of his or her special gifts, to tap and control this spiritual power.

In some tribes, the shamans' mystical powers made them somewhat feared. Among the Chumash, the shamans were seen as sorcerers as well as healers, people who could prophecy the future and were thought to perform some acts of "black" magic. If they could cure illness, they could also cause it.

As doctors, some shamans practiced bloodletting, hypnosis, and herbal medicine. But most used special rituals for healing. One ritualistic method for healing was to recover the "lost" soul of an ill person. The lost soul was believed to have wandered from the body; by calling it back, the shaman healed the body. Shamans also implemented the "singing" cure, in which the shaman sang, used a cocoon rattle, and smoked tobacco. When used in this way, tobacco was believed to have spiritual powers. The singing cure might last for several nights, during which time the shaman fasted and slept very little.

Shamans also healed by "sucking out" the cause of disease from the sick person's body. Indians believed that most illness was caused by a specific "disease" object inside the body. The shaman acted to suck out this object with a hollow pipe. Using sleight-of-hand, he produced the presumed object—a small stone, a piece of obsidian, a feather, or a small live animal like a lizard. Seeing this object, the patient often began to improve. The shaman used the patient's own belief system to encourage healing.

Both men and women could become shamans and in northwestern tribes such as the Karok, Yurok, and Hupa, shamans were generally women. The process of becoming a shaman might begin with a dream of a spiritual being, perhaps an ancestor or an animal with special powers. This dream visitor then became the Indian's guardian spirit and the source of his or her shamanistic power. In some areas of California, primarily the northwest, potential shamans had dreams in which spirits put "pains" in their bodies; they began to feel ill and to suffer. These pains were said to be minute, self-moving objects placed by a spirit into the body to cause disease. To become a shaman, a person would have to learn how to control and master the pains. More experienced shamans provided the long, rigorous training necessary to do this.

Some shamans actively sought the position. For example, a woman might try to encourage the appearance of a dream-vision by going off by herself and going without water, food, and sleep for a while. Other shamans inherited the position from their mothers or fathers. These women or men knew they would grow up to be a shaman.

The first step to becoming a shaman was to study with older, more experienced shamans. The teacher shared his or her skills with students and taught them the appropriate use of singing, music, and the sucking cure. There was an initiation rite for students, which included fasting and dancing, and ended with a special "doctor's dance," which celebrated the new shaman's position.

If a shaman failed to cure someone, he or she might be suspected of evil powers; if the shaman failed repeatedly, he or she might even be killed. If successful, the shaman was paid with food or money or valuable objects. In some groups, the patient or patient's family paid what they thought the treatment was worth, while in others shamans commanded a high fee and were paid in advance. If they couldn't cure the patient, they returned the fee. Some shamans were specialists, like the rain doctor, the rattlesnake doctor, and the bear doctor. In the deserts of southern California, rain could mean the difference between food and famine, and rain doctors were much in demand to produce rain or control the weather. Rattlesnake doctors were said to cure or prevent snakebite, a constant threat in most parts of California. Rattlesnake doctors, it was believed, could handle rattlesnakes without being bitten—and sometimes did so to prove their powers.

Bear doctors were both men and women, thought to have extraordinary powers to cure or harm. Some groups believed the bear doctor was transformed into an actual bear. When bear doctors put on the head and skin of a grizzly bear,

they were thought to take on bearlike characteristics. They became ferocious, strong, short-tempered, and gained the ability to travel quickly over long distances. Bear doctors were both respected and feared by their communities. In the Costanoan tribe, those who impersonated a bear were considered evil and were killed when discovered. In other groups, they had much status in their communities because they were thought to kill enemies of the tribe using their special powers.

BELIEFS

California Indians evolved a variety of religious practices, with traditions, special ceremonies, leaders or shamans, and rites of initiation. Anthropologists see certain patterns among these practices and have identified three main systems, which they have named the World Renewal Cult, the Kuksu, and the Jimsonweed Cult.

All of these systems had certain things in common. They were both religious and social. They were exclusive societies that conferred special status on their members. Priests,

THE WHITE DEER DANCE

The White Deer Dance, also called the Deerskin Dance, was a time for elaborate costumes. These Karok men wear shell necklaces and headdresses symbolizing deer antlers. The white deerskins that give the dance its name are in the background.

Indian of Humboldt, California
A. W. Ericson, Foto. Registered.

shamans, and other religious leaders were often members of the chief's council or held high rank in the village. They used special ceremonies to initiate the young boys into membership.

The ceremonies always involved music and dancing and took place in a special building, sometimes the sweathouse but often the community's assembly or dance house. The religion's history—an explanation of how a divine being had created it long ago—was an important part of the ceremonies. This history was transmitted through stories, songs, and dances. In most places, religious practices were male-only activities, though women were often observers at the dances.

These religious systems did not have a ruling political organization or a single, powerful leader. But the World Renewal and Kuksu systems did link together many different tribes through large ceremonial events. The host community issued invitations to peoples from neighboring tribes. Hundreds and even thousands of people took part, traveling as far as 50 miles. During the visit, they got to know each other as they swapped stories, traded, and entertained each other. The men often gambled together, spent time in the sweathouse, and competed in athletic events.

Many northwest tribes participated in what is called the World Renewal Cult. The World Renewal Indians believed that such events as lightning, earthquake, fire, or accidents were caused by supernatural forces and that regular ceremonies and rites were needed to keep these forces in check—to maintain, or renew, the world. Ceremonies were believed to keep the world on an even keel—stable and productive, with humans in control. Ceremonies protected the health and well-being of men and women and kept the woods filled with game, the rivers filled with fish, and the oak trees filled with acorns.

World Renewal ceremonies might last more than two weeks. During this time, a number of different rites, or religious activities, took place. Each rite had to be carefully carried out according to ancient traditions. The shaman recited formulas based on the words of the spirits who

◄ Hupa Indians perform the White Deer Dance in 1890. The poles these dancers hold carry skins from rare albino deer. As they dance, the participants will imitate the actions of deer.

had created the universe. A new, sacred fire might be made and certain buildings, like the sweathouse, might be symbolically "renewed" by repairing or rebuilding them. In celebration of "first fruits," the first salmon catch or acorn harvest might be eaten in a ceremonial way.

An important part of the ceremonies was to show off wealth and possessions. Only the richest men in a community had the money and power to organize the event or outfit a dancing group with elaborate costumes. For example, the dancers in the Deerskin Dance wore rare white skins from albino deer and carried long poles with strips of white or multicolored deerskin. In the Jumping Dance, dancers wore colorful headbands of woodpecker scalps.

Named for the Pomo spirit *Kuksu*, the Kuksu system was a collection of highly secret societies, more like political parties or private clubs than a religion. It was practiced among central California groups, including the Pomo, Miwok, Patwin, Maidu, Cahto, and Yuki. Kuksu emphasized exclusivity, elaborate initiation rites, expensive ceremonies, and the instruction of children. Members of Kuksu were usually responsible for organizing all the ceremonies and dances held in their community. At the heart of the religion was a belief that a spirit called Kuksu had been sent by the Creator to teach people how to hunt and cook, how to perform ceremonies, and what laws to use. After doing that, Kuksu made everyone speak a different language and sent them to different parts of the world. The Maidu had a story that explained why the Creator established secret societies and elaborate rituals:

> Until now you have let all your boys grow up like a wild tree in the mountains; you have taught them nothing; they have gone their own way. Henceforth you must bring every youth, at the proper age, into your assembly house, and cause him to be initiated into the ways and knowledge and ways of manhood. You shall teach him to worship me, and to observe the sacred dances which I shall ordain in my honor. Keep the sacred dance house, as I have told you, while the world endures. Never ne-

▶ Luiseno and Cupeno Mission Indians participate in an open air mass near San Diego around 1910. Many California Indians became Christians but also tried to preserve their own religious heritage.

glect my rites and honors. Keep the sacred rattle and the dances. Worship me in the night and in the daylight. Then shall your hills be full of acorns and nuts; your valleys shall yield plenty of grass seed and herbs; your rivers shall be full of salmon, and your hearts shall be rejoiced.

At the annual ceremony, young boys went through an initiation into the Kuksu society. The site of the ceremony moved each year so that different villages were responsible for holding the event. During a week-long ceremony, dances took place in the village's earth-covered dance lodge. The dancers, dressed in feather head-dresses and robes, with painted bodies and carrying clapper sticks, impersonated spirits, most often the one the Pomo Indians called *Kuksu*. The initiates fasted, danced, and engaged in complicated rituals. They were taught the customs and folklore of their group, the rules of shamanism, and how to perform public ceremonies.

The third great religious system evolved around the use of datura, or jimsonweed, a plant that grows in dry areas. This system is sometimes referred to using the Spanish word for datura—*toloache*. All parts of datura are poisonous and if it is not consumed in very small doses it is fatal. Throughout southern California, Indians used datura in controlled dosages as a painkiller and a hallucinogenic drug. The dried plant was ground up or the root was steeped in water. The resulting brew was drunk.

Some tribes used the datura drink informally, perhaps once a year, believing it could cure illness, encourage an undeveloped talent such as gambling or hunting, and produce a personal spiritual vision. For the Yokut, Luiseno, and Cahuilla, datura was an essential part of their formal religious ceremonies, centering around the initiation of young men into a secret religious society (Yokut women also participated in the spring ritual of drinking datura). These tribes believed that ingesting datura was a spiritual experience and would give them spiritual power. The hallucinations produced by the plant were, to them, visions of spiritual beings.

After being given datura during the initiation ceremonies, the young men danced wildly for a while before falling unconscious. When they

◄ A Diegueno man in traditional dress plays a drum at a dance ceremony in California in 1909.

▲ The Pomo Indians of California wore "Big Head" feather headdresses such as this when they performed ceremonial dances.

woke up, they reported visions of spiritual beings and events experienced in the datura coma. For a week or so following this, the young men were instructed in tribal lore and sacred knowledge. The Luiseno boys were reminded of the intimate connection between humans and the natural world:

> The earth hears you.
> The sky and the sacred mountain see you.
> If you will believe this you will grow old.
> And you will see your sons and daughters
> And you will counsel them in this manner
> When you reach your old age.

As in some of the puberty rites for young women, a ground painting—an image drawn with colored sand—was used as a teaching tool, showing important spirits and aspects of the natural world. At the end of the rite, there was a great celebration with everyone in the village dancing and singing around a large bonfire.

In summary, the religious ceremony—for all the main religious systems—had several functions. It introduced the young initiate into the ancient knowledge of the tribe. It was a social occasion, which reinforced the status of the shamans and wealthy men of the tribe. It celebrated and reestablished the tribe's continuing place in the world. And it reinforced the Indian idea of a world full of invisible powers present in the visible world, a world in which stones and sky and mountains were sacred.

CEREMONIAL LIFE
RITUAL PLANTS

◀ Tobacco was sometimes used by shamans during healing ceremonies. It was also smoked as a sleep-inducing drug.

▼ Jimsonweed, or datura, is a poisonous plant used by some southern California tribes as part of their religious ceremonies. In small doses, it produces hallucinations and comas.

DANCE

◀ A flicker feather headband, shell necklace, bone whistle, and animal skin apron make up this Miwok dance outfit.

▼ Special outfits were worn during religious ceremonies. These Miwok ceremonial headbands were made with feathers from woodpeckers and worn during the Jumping Dance.

▲ A Chumash man wears a ceremonial headdress at a modern festival.

▶ This ceremonial feather belt was used by Pomo Indians in the Jumping Dance. In this dance, participants mimic the jerky motions of a woodpecker.

▼ The brilliant red feathers from the heads of many different woodpeckers were used to make this Hupa dance headband.

◀ This Coyote Dance outfit has a coyote head and a feather robe. The dancer's white-painted legs and the white sticks he holds represent the coyote's legs.

▶ Elaborate ear plugs (a type of earring) were worn on special occasions. This ear plug, made by a Sierra Miwok, is made of feathers, beads, and shells.

▼ Pendants, necklaces, earrings, and other personal adornments were made by all the California Indians. This Sierra Miwok pendant necklace is made from abalone shell.

▲ Painted deerskin was used to make this Modoc dance
drum. The drumstick is decorated with feathers.

CHAPTER FOUR

CHANGES

For thousands of years, California Indians continued their stable lifeways. They honored their spirits, celebrated their harvests and hunts, and mourned their dead as they had for generations. But half a world away, events were unfolding that would radically alter the Indian way of life. In the late 15th century, Spain colonized the Caribbean and parts of South America and, in 1512, began sending expeditions to what is now Mexico. The immediate goal was to find a shorter trade route to China, but the Spaniards also found gold and silver in the great Indian cities of the Aztecs. The colony they founded, called New Spain, took in present-day Mexico, parts of Baja (Lower) California, and the western coast of South America. When officials began hearing rumors of fabulous cities of gold to the north, they decided to explore for riches and to look for a "northwest passage"—a waterway between the Atlantic and Pacific Oceans. They began sending sailing expeditions up the coast of Alta (Upper) California.

THE EUROPEANS ARRIVE

One of the first of these expeditions was that of

Juan Rodriquez Cabrillo. In 1542, Cabrillo and his crew set out in two small ships from the Mexican port of Navidad and became the first Europeans to see the Indians living in California. As the ships made their way along the shoreline, the men saw many Indian villages. Cabrillo gave the name "Bay of Smokes" to present-day Los Angeles because the bowl-shaped valley was filled with smoke from Indian fires.

If some of the Indians were afraid on seeing the strange European ships for the first time, others were not and eagerly came out in their canoes to greet the strangers. Seeing opportunities for trade, the Indians were friendly and offered the Spaniards fresh sardines in exchange for beads and clothing. The Cabrillo expedition was not a success, however. The Spanish found neither gold nor a northwest passage in California, Cabrillo died, and most of the crew came down with scurvy.

In 1579, the English privateer Francis Drake landed at what is now Drake's Bay, north of San Francisco, to make repairs on his ship, *The Golden Hind*. Drake and his men stayed in California for five weeks and became friendly with the local Miwok. His account also shows the Indians were not timid in their dealings with the Europeans. The day after the English arrived, one of the Miwok rowed out three times in a canoe to

▲ Years after the mission system ended, some Native Americans of southern California were still called Mission Indians. In this engraving from 1877, Indians make baskets and rope.

the ship. On the third visit, he brought a gift, which Drake described as ". . . a bunch of feathers, much like the feathers of a blacke crow, very neatly and artificially gathered upon a string, and drawne together into a round bundle; being very cleane and finely cut. . . ." Before he left, Drake claimed the land for England and put up a brass plate holding a sixpence with the image of Queen Elizabeth I. In 1602, another Spanish expedition, under the leadership of Sebastian Vizcaino, explored and mapped the California coast. Following that, there were no European visitors to Indian California for 167 years.

THE MISSION SYSTEM

In the late 18th century, Spain once again turned its attention north. The newly appointed administrator of New Spain, José de Galvez, was brilliant, vain, and ambitious. To increase profits from the colonies and build his own political power, he decided to extend Spain's territories northward to include Alta California. Playing on the Spanish fear that England and Russia wanted to take over California, Galvez proposed that Spain lay claim to California by building presidios, or forts, and founding missions there. The presidios would be a show of military strength while the missions would colonize and subdue the native population.

The job of establishing the California missions was given to the Franciscan padres, headed by Father Junipero Serra. In 1769, Serra—along with several other padres, a few soldiers, some Christianized Mexican Indians, and cattle and horses—traveled by land to what is now San Diego. The padres founded a mission at San Diego; later that year, they founded a second at Monterey. These were the first of 21 missions that eventually formed a chain from San Diego to just north of San Francisco. At the same time, Spanish soldiers began building presidios at the mission sites and elsewhere. Since the missions and forts were primarily limited to a strip of land along the coast, most of California, including its Indian inhabitants, remained independent of Spanish control.

The lure of safety, shelter, and food brought some Indians into the missions. Historian George H. Phillips suggests that others "drifted into the missions to acquire the special spiritual powers they believed the missionaries possessed. Indians were also impressed with the practical knowledge and skills the Spanish were willing to

▲ A Mission Indian woman makes lace at the Pala Mission in the 1930s.

impart." However, as nonmission Indians heard about the harshness of mission life, it became necessary to use force to produce converts. Spanish soldiers on military expeditions sometimes came into a village and simply rounded up people and took them to the mission.

The first mission buildings were rough structures of dried mud, called adobe, supported by pine beams. The roof was thatched with tule reeds, a technique borrowed from the coastal Indians. Gradually, the simple but beautiful architecture of the missions became well known. One mission padre wrote to Father Serra: "The entire aspect, especially the interior of the church and sacristy, is attractive, clean, and pleasing, because of the excellent ensemble achieved by the skill of the workers in using the resources of the mission. Thanks be to God."

The stated goal of the missions was the conversion of the Indians to Christianity, but the Indians were also essential as a source of cheap labor. The mission community not only incorporated a church, but also a working farm. Missions usually had two padres, one for religious training and the other for vocational training. The Indians worked at such trades as tile making, carpentry,

leatherwork, blacksmithing, and masonry. Indian women learned to spin yarn and weave the yarn into cloth, sew clothing, make bread from wheat flour, and make cheese and butter.

Gardens and farmlands produced vegetables, corn, beans, lentils, wheat, and barley. The grapes grown in vineyards were made into wine and brandy. When the mission fathers introduced irrigation to California, Indian labor helped produce citrus fruit, figs, dates, and olives. In 1775, a large herd of cattle and horses was driven up from Mexico; this formed the basis for a cattle ranching industry. While the cattle gave meat for eating, the hides and tallow were exported for profit.

An Indian convert was called a neophyte, meaning "beginner." This term came to be applied to all mission-dwelling Indians, even those who were born into the Catholic faith. Married Indians lived in a small village near the mission enclosure. Single men and women were strictly segregated in separate dormitories inside the mission.

Indians soon found out that residence at the mission was not voluntary. Some mission areas were hedged around with thick rows of prickly pear cactus to prevent escape. Indians who changed their minds and wanted to return to their villages and way of life were severely punished. Some Indians were put in chains, and after repeated attempts to escape, were executed. Misdemeanors of all kinds were punished by beating. Years later, a neophyte remembered:

The Indians at the mission were very severely treated by the padres, often punished by fifty lashes on the bare back. They were governed somewhat in the military style, having sergeants, corporals, and overseers who were Indians, and they reported to the padres any disobedience or infraction of the rules, and then came the lash without mercy, the women the same as the men.

The Indians did not thrive in mission life. The European diet, the absence of sanitation, and the overcrowding did not make life comfortable or healthy. The Indians had no natural immunity to diseases brought by the Spanish such as measles, smallpox, and diphtheria, and a high death rate among Indians became common. At one mission, for example, half the Indian population died within nine years.

In addition, the mission system deprived the Indians of their community life. The padres, with their own deeply held religious views, didn't acknowledge the Indians' own religious systems. They treated them like children who needed instruction. A French nobleman observed in 1786 that the mission Indian was "too much a child, too much a slave, too little a man."

INDIAN RESISTANCE

The California Indians were ill-prepared to defend themselves against the Spanish. Most California tribes were peace-loving. Even those that engaged in warfare did so sporadically and without developing a sophisticated military class. In addition, the basic social unit of the tribe was the village, which was often a small community of a hundred or so people. There was no large organized Indian group that could arm itself against the Europeans.

Yet some Indians did resist Spanish occupation. Many risked punishment and death in attempts to escape from the missions. Other Indians actively rebelled. About a month after the founding of the San Diego mission, the Indians—perhaps realizing that the Spanish were there to stay—attacked the mission. One Spaniard and several Indians were killed. In 1775, the Diegueno Indians protested the removal of the Mission San Diego to the site of one of their villages. Six hundred Indians burned the mission buildings and killed a padre. Later, they drifted back into the mission, perhaps in fear of the soldiers. In 1785, a young Gabrielino woman named Toypurina led six Indian groups in an attack at Mission San Gabriel. In 1824, at Mission La Purisma, 2,000 Indians lay siege to the mission for several months, while at nearby Santa Barbara Indians burned the mission and fled to the hills.

THE END OF THE MISSIONS

Pueblos or towns gradually grew up around the missions and presidios, settled by immigrants from Mexico, often convicts or the very poor. Meanwhile, a new class of Californios, or native Californians, was gaining power. These were the rancheros who established large ranchos, or cat-

tle ranches, on the rolling grasslands between the ocean and the coastal mountains.

The powerful rancheros had their eye on the missions' productive crops, herds of cattle, experienced cowboys, and full wine cellars. In 1820, they got their chance. After an 11-year war with Spain, Mexico declared its independence in 1820 and California became a territory of Mexico. In 1834, the Mexican government announced that the mission system would be secularized, or dismantled. The mission chapel would become the local church, with parish priests. Each Indian head of household or adult male would be given 33 acres of land as well as part of the mission's crops and cattle. The rest of the land and goods would go to ranchos. The Indians would cease to be wards of the mission and become citizens of the new towns.

Some Indians did farm their plots of land for a while and a few others were deeded rights to large ranchos. However, many Indians were not informed of their rights and others lacked adequate farming supplies, seeds, and tools. In time, most of the mission lands ended up in the hands of the Californios.

With the missions disbanded, Indians found themselves with few options. Many Indians went to work in the newly growing towns of Los Angeles, San Diego, Santa Barbara, and San Jose. These towns became very dependent on cheap Indian labor, as did the ranchos, farms, and vineyards.

Indians were so important to the Los Angeles work force that Indian prisoners were auctioned off every week to those who needed workers. To ensure a steady supply of prisoners, employers paid their Indian workers not in cash but in cheap aguardiente, or brandy. The Indians, who had never used alcohol before, drank up their weekly earnings and were then thrown in jail for drunkenness.

Other Indians went to work on the ranchos. One rancho described the Indians' place in Californio life this way:

Indians tilled our soil, pastured our cattle, sheared our sheep, cut our lumber, built our houses, paddled our boats, made tiles for our homes, ground our grain, slaughtered our cattle, dressed their hides for market, and made our unburnt bricks; while the Indian women made excellent servants, took care of our children, made every one of our meals.

◀ Mission Dolores in San Francisco was founded by the Franciscan padres in 1776. The original adobe-walled mission building was built in 1782.

On ranchos, Indians lived inside their own communities and had some degree of independence. They could practice their own religion, marry whom they wanted to, and grow their own gardens in the time left over from their rancho jobs. However, they lived at a subsistence level. They worked long, hard hours under poor conditions and were paid not in cash, but in goods—food, supplies, and clothing.

Some former mission Indians fled to the interior, where neither the mission system nor the ranchos had penetrated deeply. There they joined up with related tribes or formed new groups. While the coastal Indians had been absorbed by the mission system, the Indians of the interior had continued their way of life. These Indians had suffered only sporadic military campaigns waged by the Mexican government.

However, American trappers and hunters were making slow inroads into the interior of the state. In the 1830s and early 1840s, a few American settlers arrived overland from the east and north and settled in the lush Central Valley. At first, the number of settlers was too small to have a serious effect on the Indian population. But white communities were growing and many whites were hostile to the presence of Indians. Meanwhile, events far outside California were about to decide its political fate.

THE GOLD RUSH

In May 1846, the United States declared war on Mexico. This war revolved around land disputes in Texas, but much more was at stake. If the war were won, the United States would acquire a thousand miles of California shoreline and many excellent harbors. The country would stretch from coast to coast—a fulfillment of what was called the "Manifest Destiny" of America.

During the Mexican-American War, there were military skirmishes in California, as some Californios put up resistance for a while. They were, however, outnumbered by the U.S. troops situated there. In February 1848, Mexico declared defeat and the war was ended. Mexico signed the Treaty of Guadalupe Hidalgo giving the United States a vast tract of western lands, including parts of California. (California sought statehood in 1849 and entered the Union in 1850.) The United States got a bonus when it acquired California: Nine days before the treaty was signed, gold was found in the foothills of the Sierra Nevada range.

In the 1840s, a Swiss settler named John Sutter had established a community, a farm, and a fort near present-day Sacramento. In January 1848 one of Sutter's workers—a man named James Marshall—was building a lumber mill on the north fork of the American River when he found a lump of gold on the bottom of the icy stream. Marshall and Sutter tried to keep the discovery a secret, but word spread quickly. Gold fever hit so fast and so hard that by June 1848 the streets of San Francisco and Monterey were virtually empty. Everyone had gone to the gold fields. Among the first miners were Indians, sent by the rancheros to mine gold for them. Other Indians, living near the foothills region, looked for gold independently.

It wasn't long before the rest of the world got gold fever and began heading for California. In the spring of 1849, the first gold seekers arrived from Oregon, South America, Asia, the east coast of the United States, and Europe.

The effect of the 1849 gold rush on the Indians was devastating. Thousands of new people poured into Central Valley, the foothills, and the mountains, which had remained under Indian settlement. The forty-niners weren't settlers; they were people whose sole aim was to get rich quick and get out. Many were men (there were few women) with shady pasts who were not likely to be considerate of the rights of Indians. There was little law enforcement in the mining camps in any event. Justice was swift, brutal—and often wrong.

The rancheros had used Indians to mine for gold but the new arrivals saw Indians as a threat. In their view, all Indians were "hostile" and "savage," to be gotten rid of on the least pretext. Furthermore, they didn't like sharing the gold treasure with the Indians. Miners called the Indians "diggers." This term was applied contemptuously to the Indians because some tribes, especially in the southwest, used a stick to dig up roots and insects. No one seems to have caught the irony that the miners, who spent long days laboriously digging in the mud for gold, were also "diggers."

Violent hostilities became a fact of life for the Indians. Early in 1849, a group of Oregon miners entered a Maidu village and raped several women. Those Indians who tried to help the women were shot. The Indians later killed five miners in reprisal and the Oregonians responded by attacking and killing a dozen Indians, later executing seven more.

▲ The miners who rushed to California after gold was discovered there in 1849 scarred the land by cutting all the trees and then washing the soil away. The miner panning for gold is surrounded by a desolate landscape of mud and rock.

Indians were often blamed for crimes that they didn't commit. In 1849, five white men were discovered missing from camp. With no concrete evidence, the other miners decided that Indians were the culprits. They formed a posse and attacked an Indian village, killing 20 villagers and captured 80 more. When the Indians tried to escape, all 80 were shot.

As a result of this kind of violence, Indians soon began departing from the gold fields. In 1848, almost half the 4,000 miners were Indians; by the next year, most had fled. Some chose to live in cities or work for whites, but they soon found themselves competing for jobs with disappointed gold seekers and were eventually pushed out of the job market. Some Indians disappeared higher up into the Sierra Nevada while others migrated to the barren lands to the southeast.

Meanwhile, the cycle of violence continued. Under California law, Indians were forbidden to testify against whites. It was almost impossible, therefore, for Indian victims of white crime to get a fair trial. In 1849, Pomo Indians took the law into their own hands, killing two white ranchers because they were abusing and killing their Indian workers. The following year, a party of U.S. soldiers went looking for the Pomo at their home at Clear Lake. Although the Pomo met them in peace, the soldiers attacked. At least 135 Indians—men, women, children, and old people—were killed. Two white soldiers died. One observer said the Indians fell "as grass before the sweep of the scythe."

Many approved of these acts of random violence. The governor of California, John Mc-Dougall, told the state legislature in 1851 to expect that "a war of extermination will continue to be waged between the races until the Indian races becomes extinct. . . ."

Subsequently, a number of repressive measures were instituted against the Indians. In 1851, 1852, and 1857, the state legislature approved reimbursements to any white man who fought and killed Indians. Settlers offered bounties for Indians scalps or heads. A number of militias were formed for the purpose of killing Indians. By 1860, over 4,000 Indians had been killed in military encounters.

In 1850, the state legislature passed an act that provided for the indenturing of Indians to whites. Indenturing allows one person to be bound to another for a certain length of time, to work or to learn a trade. In California, indenturing amounted to a legitimized form of slavery.

Settlers paid up to $50 or $60 for healthy Indian children or young girls who would cook or clean for them. To ensure a supply of indentured workers, slave brokers captured Indian women and kidnapped children. Between 3,000 and 4,000 children were seized and taken from their families.

The *Sacramento Union* newspaper reported on the condition of indentured Indians, held "as slaves were held in the South; those owning them use them as they please, beat them with clubs and shoot them down like dogs, and no one to say: 'Why do you do so?' " Despite protests like this, indenturing continued to flourish until 1867, four years after slavery was abolished in the United States.

The condition of the Indians steadily deteriorated. Gold mining had begun the destruction of the Indians' resources. Digging for gold stirred up mud and silt which ruined the salmon streams and killed the rich oyster beds at the mouths of rivers. To build fast, temporary mining settlements (which often became ghost towns just as quickly), miners cut down trees; the deforested areas had no game animals and suffered mudslides and further erosion. Later on, a process called hydraulic mining, which involved spraying quantities of water on hillsides to wash down gold-filled earth, left huge scars on the landscape, destroying plants and wildlife habitats.

SETTLERS ARRIVE

Meanwhile, increasing numbers of settlers from the east displaced the Indians from their homelands. As farms sprang up, valuable hunting and gathering lands were lost. Larger game such as deer and elk fled. The abundant oak trees were felled to clear pastures and build houses, while farmers fed the acorns to their hogs. Crops were planted where staples of Indian food such as grasses, fruits, and wild plants had once flourished. Many Indians were literally starving to death.

In order to feed themselves, some began to steal livestock from the large ranches. They had become good raiders during the Spanish and Mexican periods, and now they made forays onto ranches to take cattle and horses for eating. This set off more violent reprisals from whites. Cattle ranchers, vigilantes, and army units attacked and killed entire Indian villages. In 1856, the *Sacramento Union* newspaper wrote about the Indian cattle raids, saying that "the fault has been with

the whites. The herds of cattle said to have been stampeded turn out to a single calf taken to supply the deficiency of meat during an Indian feast. [What follows is] retaliation, of a brutal character, for this trifling offense."

The diseases of the whites continued to cause major epidemics among the Indians. Thousands died from smallpox, measles, diphtheria, and venereal disease. Starvation, malnutrition, alcoholism, and psychological stress also took their toll.

Governor McDougall's goal of extermination of the Indians was being achieved, slowly and painfully. The reduction in the numbers of California Indians during the 1800s was drastic. When the missionaries arrived in 1769, there were about 310,000 Indians living in California. By 1900, the Indian population had been cut by more than 90 percent, to 20,000.

Despite disease, starvation, and displacement, there were still Indians in California. In most whites' view, they were undesirable and unwanted. Even those sympathetic to the Indians believed that progress and settlement would gradually and inevitably wipe out the Indians and their way of life. Indians were occupying land that whites wanted for mining, grazing, farming, and settling. They were fishing waters that whites wanted to divert for irrigation. No one—except the Indians themselves—recognized that the Indians had a right to the land they had occupied for thousands for years. But what could be done?

• THE RESERVATION SYSTEM

In 1850, a commission was established by the federal government to study the problem. The commissioners proposed a reservation system based on 18 treaties, which would give the Indians over seven million acres of land, about eight percent of the total area of the state. However, the treaties were voted down by the state legislature, which objected both to so much land going to the Indians and to making a large part of the Indian labor pool unavailable.

In 1852, Edward F. Beale was appointed superintendent of California's Indian Service. He

RESERVATION LIFE

The office and general store at the Round Valley Agency in Mendocino County, California, in 1876. White squatters killed 45 Indians here. This reservation exists today.

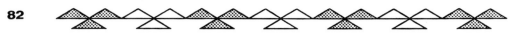

proposed a more moderate reservation system with a total of 1,250,00 acres. From the start, the reservation system had problems. Indians were not given the tools or training to become self-sustaining. They didn't receive medical care, farming supplies, or much-needed food. In addition, the Indian Service too often failed to offer legal advice to Indians or protect them against white squatters. Officials sometimes didn't visit reservations for months on end.

Fraud and corruption further marred the reputation and policies of the Indian Service. Corrupt officials racked up high debts while in office and left them unpaid. Beef that was supposed to be delivered to starving Indians was sold instead to miners. Employees or white squatters who abused the Indians went unpunished. Even rounding up Indians for the reservations could become a cover for further violence. In some places, military expeditions ambushed Indian villages at night. Those who survived the attack were removed to the reservation.

Generally, Indian reservations were sited on land that whites didn't want, with poor soil, little water, and no game to hunt. Increasing the problem was that land set aside for reservations was usually not on the Indians' homeland. As the *Sacramento Union* noted in 1859, ". . . the Indian is known to be particularly attached to his childhood home, and as long as any of his kindred remain he will . . . eventually return to his early stamping ground. . . ."

One tribe that resisted being transported to a reservation was the Hupa. They fought for five years and in 1864 were given a reservation on their own homelands in the Hoopa Valley, where they made a successful transition to a farming economy.

THE MODOC WAR

Another tribe that resisted was the Modoc. The Modoc were told to leave their home on the Lost River, although this land, primarily high and barren, was undesirable from the whites' point of view. (It is still relatively unoccupied.) Nevertheless, the Modoc were forcibly marched to a reservation on Klamath territory in southern Oregon. Led by their leader, Kintpuash, many of the Modoc deserted the reservation and returned to their home on the Modoc Plateau. In the winter of 1872–73, an armed force of 1,000 soldiers attacked 150 Modoc who were hiding out in the lava beds. For a while, the Modoc successfully

▲ Scarfaced Charley (Chichikam Lupalkuelatko) fired the first shots of the Modoc War in November, 1872. He was the chief military strategist for the Indians.

resisted. During one negotiation, Kintpuash killed a U.S. general and a minister. The Modoc War, as it was called, cost the United States 75 soldiers and half a million dollars. Eventually, the Modoc were defeated and Kintpuash and three other rebellion leaders were executed.

THE GHOST DANCE MOVEMENT

With increasing numbers of whites coming to California, even reservations ceased to be a safe haven. White squatters moved onto reservation lands, diverting water from the reservation, and stealing Indian livestock. The whites' cattle overran Indian crops and ate acorns. White lumber mills were allowed to operate on reservations, even though they polluted salmon streams. At

▲ Kintpuash, also known as Captain Jack, led the Modoc in resisting forced emigration to a reservation in Oregon. The Modoc lost the so-called Modoc War and Kintpuash was executed on October 3, 1873.

▲ The steam and natural lava trenches of the Modoc Plateau's volcanic landscape made it possible for a small number of Modoc to hold off a large number of soldiers during the Modoc War.

Round Valley reservation, for example, a group of white squatters told the Indians to get off or be killed. Forty-five Indians were massacred and the white squatters were allowed to remain. One estimate is that four-fifths of Round Valley was illegally occupied by whites.

In the 1870s, some Indians in northern and central California turned for help to a religious movement called the Ghost Dance. (This new religion is not the same as the ghost dances many California Indians performed to honor their dead.) The leaders of the Ghost Dance religion said that the time was coming when life would be as it was before the coming of the whites. They said the ghosts of the dead would came back, Indians would reclaim their homelands, and whites would disappear. The Ghost Dance was a powerful movement for a short time, because it offered a glimpse of hope to suffering Indians.

FAILURE OF THE RESERVATIONS

It was becoming increasingly clear to many that the reservation system was failing. The small reservation farms offered only a subsistence level economy and Indians were forced to work at low-paying jobs off the reservation, where they were often cheated out of their wages or paid in cheap whiskey. Bad food, outright starvation, overcrowding, the absence of health care, and poverty combined to produce disease and a high mortality rate. In 1884, special Indian agent Helen Hunt Jackson wrote a book called *Ramona*, which described the condition of the Cahuilla under white expansion. While it drew national attention to the plight of Indians, it did little to

▲ Toby Riddle, also known by her Modoc name of Winema, was a cousin of Kintpuash. She and her husband, a white man named Jack Riddle, acted as peacemakers during the Modoc War. Here Toby Riddle stands in the center; Jack Riddle is on her left.

help the problems. Because of the corruption of the reservation system and the difficulty of making a living, many Indians deserted the reservations. Those who stayed were prevented from keeping their Indian traditions and culture. Reservation officials prohibited Indian dances and feasts and were told to discourage long hair or face painting. Indians who objected were punished by not receiving government supplies or rations.

In the 1880s, day schools and boarding schools were introduced on the reservations. Most Indians saw, correctly, that the white-run schools were yet another attempt to destroy their language and lifeways. Indian languages were prohibited in schools. Many children were forced to leave home and go to boarding schools. Harsh discipline was often the rule and students were forced to take part in an "outing system," which placed them in low-paying domestic jobs after school. Indians protested by occasionally burning school buildings.

In 1895, a schoolteacher was murdered. The question of land ownership continued to be a problem. In 1887, the Dawes Act, or Allotment Act, called for the breakup and distribution of communally held Indian lands and resources into individual allotments of land. Heads of households would receive 80 acres of farmland

or 160 acres of grazing land. The Indians resisted allotment, fearing that it would further destroy tribal homelands and tribal identity. Years later, the top administrator at the Bureau of Indian Affairs supported this view when he said that the Dawes Act had been "principally an instrument to deprive Indians of their lands." Nationally, Indians lost two-thirds of their reservation land because of the Dawes Act. But in California, the act was less effective and only about one-fourth of Indian land was lost. In fact, some public lands were converted into allotments—a total of nearly 2,500 rancherias, or homesites.

In 1888, the Cupeno Indians were ousted from their land at Warner's Hot Springs. They brought their case before the California State Supreme Court, arguing that their land had been given to them as part of a Mexican land grant. The court had upheld the legitimacy of Mexican land grants, but in 1901 the United States Supreme Court ruled against the Cupeno. The Cupeno were able to find a new homesite at Pala Valley, through the actions of the Sequoya League, formed by a group of influential Los Angeles citizens. But they had lost their homelands.

In 1924, partly as a result of Indian's valorous service in World War I, all Indians born in the United States were granted citizenship. Prior to this time, most Indians had not been able to vote or hold office.

During the depression of the 1930s, Indians were among those hardest hit. But the 1930s also saw better legislation for Indians. In 1934, the Indian Reorganization Act repealed the Dawes Act and ended allotments. The act aimed at giving Indians more control over reservation business, provided for loans to stimulate Indian economy, and encouraged better health and education services.

One critical issue for many Indians was reimbursement for lands lost to white settlement. In the 1920s, activist groups such as the California Indian Brotherhood, the Mission Indian Federation, and the California Indian Rights Association campaigned to sue the government for the 18 unratified treaties of 1852, which would have ensured more than seven million acres to Indians. The suit took 16 years and in 1944, the Indians (descendants of those affected in the 19th century) were awarded about $5 million. This amounted to about $150 per person, or less than a dollar per acre.

A second claim for reimbursement was begun under the Indian Claims Act of 1946. This claim

asked for compensation for all land not affected by the 1946 settlement, the Mexican land grants, and other reservations—about 64,500,000 acres. Eighteen years later, a settlement was reached in which Indians were awarded $29.1 million, or $700 per person.

THE TERMINATION ERA

In 1945, Dillon Myer, who as head of the War Relocation Administration was responsible for the internment of Japanese in this country during World War II, became head of the Bureau of Indian Affairs. Myer's goal for the BIA was not the preservation of tribal lifeways or the encouragement of Indian self-determination. It was the assimilation of Indians into the mainstream of American society. A major decision in support of this goal was the policy of "termination."

The purpose of termination, which began in 1947, was to eliminate the Indians' special status of living on federally controlled and protected land. Under termination, Indians would be subject to state law, including property taxation. Federal health services, as well as utilities and educational services, would be ended. Certain rights—for example, to hunt and to fish the

▲ Starting in the 1880s, many Indian children were sent away from their families to boarding schools. These girls were students at the Perris Indian School in 1905. The girls on the left are very young, perhaps only four or five.

land—might be lost. The land itself was affected. Under termination, some communally held tribal lands were broken up and sold. Other lands and resources were once again to be divided into individual allotments, as under the Dawes Act.

Indians protested that they needed federal health care services and aid to education and that property taxes would place a burden on their already depressed economy. They also argued that termination would further undermine tribal sovereignty and erode tribal land. The process, however, went ahead. Federal health programs were transferred to the state in 1955. But state and county services often couldn't fill the gap and it was not until 1967 that the California Indian Health Project brought adequate public health services back to reservation Indians.

The termination policy proceeded for over a decade and affected about 110 Indian groups, from small bands to large tribes. Throughout the 1950s, it became clear that termination was not

▲ This 1904 photograph shows hopeful land purchasers at an auction of the California Development Company, which irrigated the Colorado Desert and renamed it the Imperial Valley. The Indians who had lived there were forced off the land.

succeeding. States didn't want the extra financial burden, Indians continued to oppose the policy, and the costs of implementing the program rose. In 1960, termination ground to a halt and Congress restored the tribal status of some western Indian groups. In addition to termination, Myer had developed a program to relocate reservation Indians to large cities where housing and job opportunities would be better—at least theoretically. The relocation program dramatically affected the Indian population of California. Until 1950, that population had remained at around 20,000 Indians. Between 1960 and 1980, Indians relocating from other parts of the country swelled it by almost 160,000. In 1980, more Indians lived in Los Angeles than in any other large city in the country.

LIFE TODAY

Some Indians today speak of a spirit of "pan-Indianism," which stresses a shared heritage and intertribal cooperation. But the growing Indian population of California does not automatically solve the problems faced by many California-born Indians.

The original population of Indian California before the arrival of the whites was about 310,000. Disease, starvation, and open hostilities extinguished entire tribes and left only remnants of others. Not only tribes and languages were lost, but shared beliefs and old ways of doing things. Indians were dispersed throughout California society. Families and communities were often too scattered to offer support or promote traditions.

Yet despite these great difficulties, there has been a surge of social activism among surviving tribes. The Yurok fought for their fishing rights along the Klamath River. The Santa Barbara Indians protested putting a supertanker terminal on their shoreline. In 1969, a coalition of 300 Indians called the Indians of All Tribes protested and publicized poor reservation conditions by occupying Alcatraz Island—a deserted prison site—for two years. The group compared a typical Indian reservation with Alcatraz, pointing out that both had inadequate sanitation facilities, no health care or educational facilities, rocky and nonproductive soil, no adequate transportation system, no fresh water, no oil or mineral rights, no industry, and high unemployment.

There is new pride today in tribal identity. In 1964, Cahuilla tribal leader Rupert Costo organized the American Indian Historical Society, which called for changes in the public school

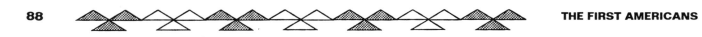

textbooks of California, giving a clearer and less distorted account of Indian life and history. In the 1970s, the Cupa Cultural Center at Pala was founded by the Cupeno and the Malki Museum in Riverside County was established as a home for Cahuilla artifacts. Also in the 1970s, the Pomo Ya-Ka-Ma project offered practical training in modern farm technology and held a traditional "first fruits" celebration in the spring.

Ancient beliefs and activities—such as dances, games, feasts, and funerals—are being restored. Historian James J. Rawls recounts that the Achomawi of northern California "have maintained an extensive knowledge and use of aboriginal medicines, foods, and rituals. Their faith in their shamans remains strong and they still know

the location of 'power places,' isolated spots in their traditional territory, where one may go to seek supernatural power."

Today, California Indians call for stronger vocational training, more educational and employment opportunities, better-paying jobs, and improved services for reservation and rural Indians. Many say that self-determination—a more powerful voice in reservation policies as well as state and local politics—is essential to finding solutions to social problems. The Indian spirit has survived much, they say, and must endure.

▼ In 1969, a coalition of Indians from many tribes occupied Alcatraz Island in San Francisco Bay in a protest against their treatment by the government.

INDIAN CULTURE IN CALIFORNIA
CONTEMPORARY ART

▲ In this mask Hupa artist George Blake combines the traditional (a wolf headdress) with the modern (a present-day Indian wearing sunglasses).

THE SPANISH INFLUENCE

One of the first Europeans to encounter the Native Americans of California was Juan Rodriquez Cabrillo, who sailed along the coast in 1542. A monument marks the place where he landed, near what is now the city of San Francisco.

The first mission in Calfornia was established in 1769 in San Diego. Others, such as San Juan Bautista, followed soon after. At first, the Native Americans came willingly to the missions, but harsh treatment soon made them wary.

The mission system grew to include 21 missions stretching from San Diego in the south to north of San Francisco. Mission San Juan Capistrano was built, using Indian labor, in the late 1700s.

▲ A Miwok woman demonstrates how to split pine branchlets in preparation for making a coiled basket.

MODERN LIFE

▶ Today Native Americans are working hard within their communities to overcome the serious family problems many face.

▼ At an Indian festival, some participants dance while others (on the left) provide the beat using clappers made of wood. In the background is a temporary shelter made of branches in the traditional style.

ASK ME ABOUT FOSTER PARENTING

INDIAN CHILD AND FAMILY SERVICES

PROTECT OUR CHILDREN

▲ Contemporary celebrations of Native American life
provide an opportunity for non-Indians to learn about
Indian lifeways. Here, a young girl tries on a deer-hunt-
ing headdress.

INDEX

PICTURE CREDITS